MARLA C. BERNS

With contributions by
MICHAEL DARLING
KURT G. F. HELFRICH

PAUL TUTTLE DESIGNS

University Art Museum
University of California,
Santa Barbara

(Half title)
The Weed, 1971
Steel, paint

(Title page)
Paul Tuttle in the Strässle
showroom, 1997

CONTENTS

6   **Preface**
EUDORAH M. MOORE

8   **Acknowledgments**
MARLA C. BERNS

12   **Paul Tuttle: A Lifelong Search for the Essence**
MARLA C. BERNS

132   **Cosmopolitan Conversations:
The Furniture Designs of Paul Tuttle**
MICHAEL DARLING

158   **The Architectural Projects of Paul Tuttle**
KURT G. F. HELFRICH

184   **Paul Tuttle: Biography and Bibliography**

188   **Photography Credits**

I first met Paul Tuttle in the early 1960s when we were introduced by a mutual acquaintance. We soon became friends in that amazing way that Paul had of creeping into your consciousness and then your affection. Southern California at this time was an unusual and exciting environment. An influx of European refugees, intellectuals, musicians, artists, and authors had culturally enriched the area in the years surrounding the Second World War. And a wave of GI's had taken up residence on these sunny shores upon their return from active duty.

Filled with idealism and determined ideas of building a better world, these former servicemen bore with them a pervasive optimism. The passage of the GI Bill—embraced by so many—proved a transformative event. It enhanced the offerings of the already broad California educational system and lent it vitality. The slightly older, more mature students who flooded the state's institutions of higher learning made informed decisions regarding their studies and were determined not to be trapped in what they saw as the mundane patterns of their parents' lives. This led many to a captivation with the arts. At the same time crafts began to move out of trade and technical schools and into colleges, away from an emphasis on artisanship and materials and toward more conceptual explorations. The whole field of industrial design was just emerging and being recognized. The lines between the disciplines seemed less rigid. Possibilities appeared endless. This was the roiling climate of the time, and it was in the midst of this heady milieu that Paul planted himself.

Determined not to return to the stultifying life he had left, Paul, in an amazing act of courage, decided to pursue his unique vision of what he wanted to accomplish, of who he wanted to be. He set out on the path to becoming his own invention—a path from which he never veered. Though he was fully aware of the sacrifices, anxieties, and hardships his choice would entail, there was never a question in his mind as to what he had to do. This determination and constancy invested his work with a special seriousness and meaning, a character and energy that was palpable.

From the moment he made his decision, his life advanced profoundly forward, his values deeply held. Rough roads, rocky slopes, yes, plenty, but the course was always onward. Wonderfully for us—and also for his designs—this straight arrow had giggly edges and an extremely compassionate core. Design superseded ambition, and he could not bend to accommodate what he felt to be negative compromises. Alterations of line or material purely to make fabrication cheaper or easier were unthinkable if they impinged on the visual integrity of the piece. Workmanship, finish, perfection as he saw them constituted universal truths and must be honored.

As curator of design at the Pasadena Art Museum, I saw his work frequently and was impressed by its innate elegance, unvarying quality, and the thoughtful solutions he had arrived at. Feeling that he merited broader exposure, I invited him to have an exhibition. The experience of working with Paul on the installation gave me fascinating insight into the cerebral quality of his design process. With a limited budget, he chose to divide the large gallery space into smaller segments by hanging curtains of chain mail as dividers, setting off the sections, yet allowing for a sense of the whole. I still remember our weeks of work with pleasure. Later, as I saw his subsequent exhibitions, I realized the depth and fecundity of his design solutions, for it was not the design of objects alone I was looking at but also design as a totality, as an inherent part of life.

Though he disclaimed intellectualism, his work was deeply informed and considered. Though he walked alone, he was acutely aware of the time and of what was happening internationally in the worlds of art, architecture, and design. One felt the outside world being constantly evaluated and filtered into his consciousness. New ideas were absorbed and refined. Over the years you could see his thoughts reworked, more finely honed, and developed. Because of the way he saw, conversation with him was always fun and "chewable." There were always new and unexpected things to contemplate after visiting with him.

The last exhibition of Paul's work at the University Art Museum, Santa Barbara, and the publication of this book represent a culmination and a recognition of a life truly dedicated to design. Though he liked to say that he was genetically incapable of learning other tongues—and though his extreme modesty would certainly have caused him to deny it—it is clear that in the language of design, he achieved a fluency of the highest order.

EUDORAH M. MOORE
Former Curator of Design
Pasadena Art Museum

ACKNOWLEDGMENTS

I met Paul Tuttle shortly after I moved to Santa Barbara in 1992 to assume the directorship of the University Art Museum at the University of California, Santa Barbara. He introduced himself to me at a museum event and soon after called to arrange what would be the first of many dinners and conversations. It was remarkable to meet someone of his age possessed of such incredible energy and enthusiasm. His youthfulness astounded me. He recounted wonderful stories of his travels to Europe, his early days in Santa Barbara, his annual sojourns in Switzerland. He also frequently talked about the challenges he faced as a self-taught designer and would often excitedly describe a new commission and what he was trying to achieve. His memory was admirable as was the combination of his intensity, his focus, and his overwhelming humility.

Paul was also an amazing creature of habit—you could easily predict the clothes he would wear and the food he would order. He was fiercely disciplined, and his friends often teased him about his strict "Tuttle time" and "Tuttle routines." Structure grounded him, giving the tempo of his days a regularity that he required. Paradoxically this very structure set him free and gave him license to be creative and open, responsive to the world, often seeing things most of us failed to notice.

Sometime around 1995, after our friendship had grown over a period of several years, Paul asked me if I would be his biographer. Although well known in Santa Barbara, the story of his life and work needed to be told to a larger audience. There had been three major exhibitions of his work in Santa Barbara—in 1978 at the Santa Barbara Museum of Art; in 1987 at the University Art Museum; and in 1995 at the Santa Barbara Contemporary Arts Forum.

My personal commitment to Paul Tuttle was also an institutional one. The University Art Museum is distinguished by the important Architecture and Design Collection, founded in 1963 by the late David Gebhard, the Museum's former director and curator of the collection. Gebhard had praised Tuttle's architectural projects in the book *Santa Barbara Architecture* (Santa Barbara: Capra Press, 1975) and helped organize the Museum's exhibition of Tuttle's work in 1987 along with then-curator Phyllis Plous. At that time, several pieces of furniture were given to the Museum by the artist. In 1996 we established the "Friends of Paul Tuttle Fund" to support the effort to mount a retrospective exhibition, produce a monograph on the designer's life and work, and build and sustain an archive of his furniture and original drawings, all as a lasting legacy. Paul's impact on the Santa Barbara community could be measured by the number of people eager to support this effort and by the fact that Paul could claim many of them as friends as well as patrons. Although their level of support may have varied, they were united in the degree of enthusiasm they demonstrated for the Museum's goals. I am especially grateful to the members of the "Friends of Paul Tuttle" Steering Committee for their assistance with the Museum's fundraising efforts: Michele Andina, Candice and Farshid Assassi, Suzanne Duca, Andy Neumann, and Brian and Joanne Rapp.

Very warm thanks to all the "Friends of Paul Tuttle" project sponsors: (Founding "Friends" are indicated with an asterisk), *Benefactors*: Suzanne Duca* and Reece Duca*, Lois Tuttle Hoegeman and family; Lillian and Jon B. Lovelace*, Harriet Tuttle Weber and family, University Art Museum Council; *Patrons*: Joan and Bill Crawford*, Margaret Dent*, Ann and Bob Diener*, Priscilla Giesen*, Mary and Robert Looker, Marion D. March Foundation*, Joanne and Brian Rapp*, Maria and Alex Strässle*, Jeanne C. Thayer*, Carol Lapham Valentine*; *Friends:* Nancy and Jesse Alexander*, Andina Family*, Candy and Farshid Assassi*, Gail and Barry Berkus*, Carey Berkus*, Marla Berns*, Susan Bower, Sandra Canada, Marni and Michael Cooney, Nancy Doll*, Mercedes Eichholz, Mandy and Clifford Einstein, Julia C. Emerson*, Jean and Howard Fenton*, Lauren and Rogers Flannery, Georgia and Ted Funsten*, Alma and Paul Gray*, Isabelle Greene*, Esther Grether*, Lily Guild and Anthony Slayter-Ralph*, Jill and Barry Kitnick, Ann and Joseph Koepfli*, Eudorah and Anson Moore*, Yvonne and Andy Neumann*, Ellen and Walter Newman*, Luise M. Phelps*, Zola and John Rex*, Ann and Albert Robbins*, Joan and James Tanner*, Evan and Paul Turpin, Yvonne Youmans, Valerie and Scott Youmans*; *Donors:* Anonymous, Mr. and Mrs. Ernst Beyeler, Virginia and Timothy Bliss, Ann Bronstein, Mr. and Mrs. Lynn Cadwell, Bank Ehinger and Co. Ltd, Rollin Fortier and Hilary Brace, Robert Grant, Carol and Fred Kenyon, Kathy Kreisler, Serena and Paul Kusserow, David F. Myrick, Elly and Jack Nadel, Susette H. H. C. Naylor, Yelda and Paul Recsei, Paul A. Roberts and Merrily Pebbles, Ro and Rick Sanders, Betty and Stanley Sheinbaum, Stephen and Alix Stecker, Eloise Swenson, Wilmuth Tannahill, and Marsha and William Wayne.

The retrospective exhibition *Paul Tuttle Designs* was mounted in 2001–2002 at the University Art Museum and was accompanied by a small publication. I was proud to have curated this important summary of a truly remarkable career. Before his death in July 2002 Paul told me that this exhibition "completed the circle" for him. Despite his modesty, he was able to perceive the scale and scope of what he had accomplished. For assistance with the exhibition I am very grateful to Robin Donaldson (AIA), architect and principal of the Santa Barbara/Los Angeles firm of Shubin + Donaldson Architects, who generously designed the installation in collaboration with Paul Prince, the Museum's chief designer. Donaldson's installation allowed the work to be seen to its advantage in a highly distinctive and sympathetic environment. Special thanks also go to Farshid Assassi, Michael Darling, Suzanne Duca, Esther Grether, Patrick Hall (Design Associates), Wayne McCall, Lorie Porter, Marvin Rand, Jeanne Spencer (Idea Engineering), Alex and Maria Strässle, Bud Tullis, and Unistrut for their invaluable contributions. The members of the University Art Museum staff did their usual fine work in making the exhibition a reality. Kurt Helfrich, Curator of the Architecture and Design Collection, is to be noted for organizing the presentation of Tuttle's architectural career.

The process of producing this book has also been collaborative—a work-in-progress that evolved over several years of discussion with Paul and those who worked with him. In 1997 Paul and I took a research trip to Switzerland to document what had been a central part of his life for over twenty-five years. We were accompanied by architect Andy Neumann, architectural photographer Farshid Assassi and his wife, Candice, and multilingual translator and Swiss resident Michele Andina. All "Friends of Paul Tuttle," together we retraced Paul's footsteps and saw many of the places where he had lived and worked. We traveled from the Italian- to the French- to the German-speaking parts of the country. A high point of our journey was visiting Incella, the tiny hill town overlooking Lake Maggiore where Paul lived for many years while he was working for Strässle International in Kirchberg, a train ride away. The house he lived in had stunning views of the lake and was a reminder of how strong a role nature played as inspiration for his work. Farshid Assassi extensively photographed and videotaped Paul, and I audiotaped his comments and reminiscences. After we returned, I continued the interview process and accumulated over seven hours of taped conversations, excerpts of which are included in my essay, which forms the first chapter of this book. I would like to thank my companions on that trip as well as the individuals in Switzerland whom I was fortunate to be able to interview: Maria and Alex Strässle and Esther Grether. They, along with Valerie and Scott Youmans, opened their homes and offices to us, giving us access to Tuttle's design projects and commissions.

A long list of individuals provided essential assistance and support in the research and writing of this book. Master craftsman Bud Tullis, curator of design Eudorah Moore, and architect Thornton Ladd all generously agreed to be interviewed. Suzanne Duca provided crucial help in the project's early stages, organizing the large archive of Tuttle documentary materials that I had accumulated, doing bibliographic work, and helping to catalog all of the artist's known furniture designs. At the University Art Museum, Education Curator Niki Dewart and Curatorial Assistant Elizabeth Mitchell assisted with the compilation of Tuttle's biography and bibliography. The essay, completed after I left the Museum, had many astute readers, starting with Paul Tuttle, who was humbled by the amount of ink spilled on his account but content with the results. His careful reading corrected errors of fact and interpretation. I am also very grateful to the individuals who carefully reviewed drafts of the text and offered sage advice: Eudorah Moore, Michael Darling, Andy Neumann, and Joan Tanner. Heartfelt thanks go to my Santa Barbara friends who supported me in the completion of the project after my move to Los Angeles and in the final months of Paul's life: David Robertson, Candice and Farshid Assassi, Joan Tanner, Bud Tullis, and Andy Neumann.

The other authors in this volume have infused their words with a profound respect and admiration for Paul Tuttle and his work: Michael Darling, who has written an astute appraisal of Tuttle's place within the history of twentieth-century design; Kurt Helfrich, who has done a careful and thoughtful overview of his architectural projects and early mentors; and Eudorah Moore, who has shared her candid firsthand experience of Tuttle's designs and Paul himself during the exciting period of the 1960s in Los Angeles.

This book has benefited from the talents of a wonderful production team: Lynne Kostman, who edited the essays with great sensitivity and a remarkable eye for detail; Farshid Assassi, whose gorgeous studio photographs reveal his special understanding and deep appreciation of Paul's designs and intentions; and Lorraine Wild, who has so stunningly captured the spirit and substance of Paul's work in her handsome book design . Additional photographs were generously provided by Wayne McCall, Marvin Rand, Strässle International, and others who are duly acknowledged in the photography credits. The book's final stages of production were ably overseen by UAM staff. Special thanks to Niki Dewart for her commitment to the project and to Bonnie G. Kelm, Director, Christopher Scoates, Chief Curator, and Kurt Helfrich for helping see the book to fruition.

Paul was the first to say that he was lucky in his life. He had lived in the house of his dreams, one he designed for himself at the top of a canyon in Santa Barbara with astonishing views of the ocean beyond. He was discriminating in all of his choices, from cool cars to well-made clothes to excellent food and wine. He undersold his furniture and gave pieces away to his friends; he designed new commissions for next to nothing. He lived his life with minimal compromise and maximal experience. But luck is never groundless. Paul gave so much to so many of his friends, patrons and, admirers. His talent and humanity found their rewards. With this volume I hope that he will receive, albeit posthumously, the recognition he deserves as one of the finest and most distinctive designers of the late twentieth century.

MARLA C. BERNS
Los Angeles, 2003

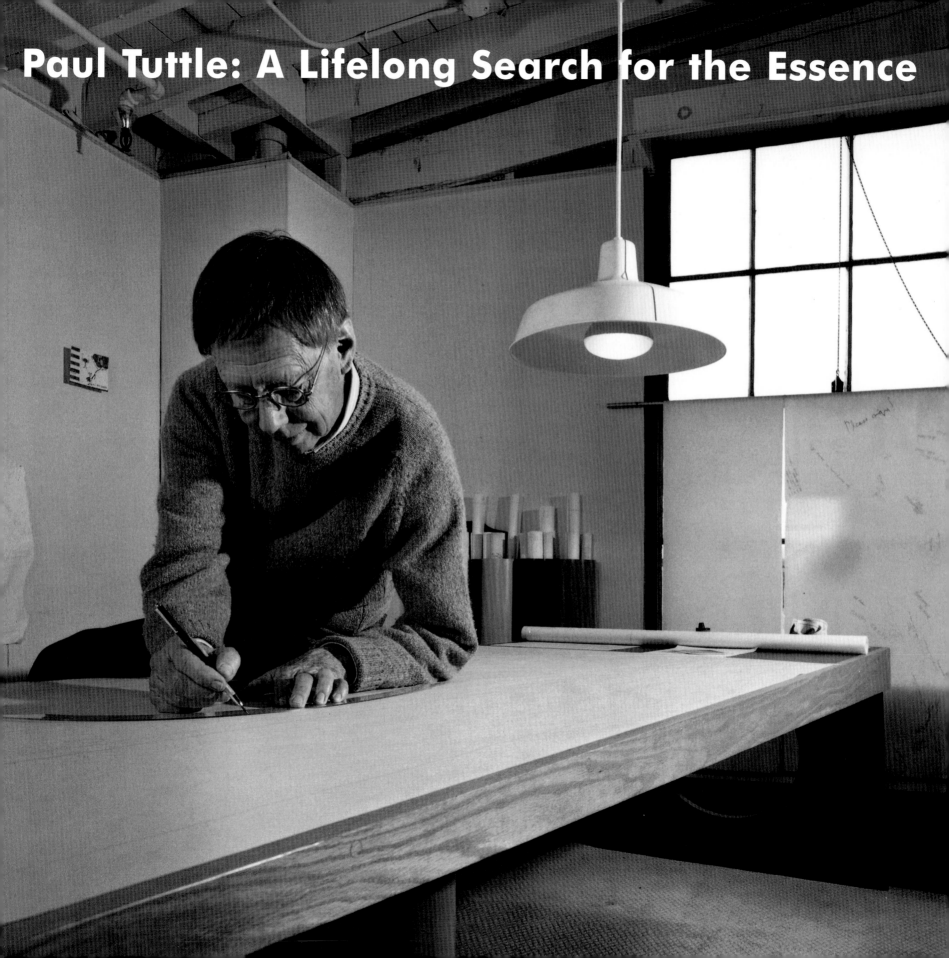

Paul Tuttle: A Lifelong Search for the Essence

MARLA C. BERNS

To possess an essence of a thing is that rare time when you can bring something to full fruition, a full sense of realization. Paul Tuttle, 2001

Paul Tuttle (1918–2002) spent fifty years engaged in the exploration of design. Although he disavowed specific goals or the desire for a particular kind of success, he possessed a remarkably clear notion of the kind of work he wanted to do—work that was uniquely his own and that met his rigorous standards of authenticity in spirit and intent. He generated designs that challenged him to solve specific structural problems, and he never easily achieved their resolution. Only toward the end of his life did he regard several of his furniture designs as "finished," when they had achieved something he considered "an essence," or a bare minimum in form, material, and structure relative to their intended purpose.

It is impossible, when summarizing such a career, to separate the creative output from the complex set of ideas, values, and intentions that form the impetus of the creativity itself. Tuttle's design career must thus be understood against the life that shaped it, from his early Midwestern years to his independent pursuit of an unconventional education attained through travel and personal encounters. This biographical sketch aims to knit together the artist's life and his work, examining the complex patterns in which they intertwine.

Paul Tuttle felt an intense need to comprehend the world in his own way, and the unique path he pursued had at its core a deep-seated faith in self-education. His temperament was a mix of stubborn determination, humility, and expressive joyfulness, traits that informed his designs as well. He had an almost boundless sensitivity to the world around him, whether responding to the simple beauty of nature, the grandeur of architectural monuments, or the precociousness of youths. His artistic sensibility ran deep, and his generosity was profound—artists, designers, and creative people were drawn to him and respected him not only for the quality of his work but also for his commitment to the power of good design to help shape the ways in which we experience the world. He was nourished by these relationships and the knowledge they could provide. His determination, autonomy, and modesty defined him and his creative work as well. His designs are singular in their clarity of form, elegance of material, and vitality of spirit. Yet, no matter how beautiful or freshly inventive, they were always, and above all, intended to be functional. Creating them was his primary enterprise—one that occupied him until the final days of his life.

Probably no other mid- to late-twentieth-century designer has had as fertile, original, and consistently accomplished a career as Paul Tuttle, and sadly his achievements remain underrecognized. His reluctance to seek fame and his unwillingness to compromise meant that success in the conventional sense was difficult to attain. Despite the formal relationships that can be drawn between his work and that of other twentieth-century designers—relationships that Michael Darling examines in chapter 2 of this volume—Tuttle's oeuvre is dominated by a passionate commitment to solving design problems in an original way. He stood out for his dogged pursuit of his own "voice" and his avoidance of trends and styles. His hundreds of designs for seating and tables are testimony to the restlessness of his creative spirit. Although he certainly admired other designers, applauding and even adopting some of their innovations, the forward progress of Paul Tuttle's career was driven by an insistence on making each piece of furniture a unique expression. The singularity and focus of his artistic vision are equally evident in his designs for houses and for total interiors, considered down to the smallest details. Although humbled by his lack of formal training, he had the confidence to trust in his own intuition, which continuously informed the distinctive achievements of his long career.

1.1 Paul Tuttle at the Design Source,
Santa Barbara, California, 1992

1.2 Paul Tuttle at the age of eleven shown seated behind his model of Charles Lindbergh's *Spirit of Saint Louis.*

1.3 This photograph of Paul Tuttle was taken while he was stationed at Scott Air Force Base in Illinois during World War II.

Paul Tuttle was born in Springfield, Missouri, in 1918. His father made his living establishing YMCAs in small towns. When Paul was quite young, the family moved to Galatin, Missouri, and his father became ill. At the recommendation of the local physician, the family moved to Saint Louis to seek better medical care. The condition was diagnosed as Parkinson's disease, and Paul's mother was forced to hold several jobs in order to support the family. In Saint Louis, Paul led an introspective childhood in austere surroundings. He and his two sisters shared in the responsibilities of maintaining the household. One of his greatest joys—and escapes—as a youth was watching airplanes fly in and out of Lambert Field, which was relatively close to his home. He was attracted to the solitary nature of flying as well as the magic of escaping into "the great unknown." Tuttle would later describe Charles Lindbergh's return to Saint Louis after his transatlantic triumph in 1927 as one of the most memorable events of his childhood (fig. 1.2). In 1941 Tuttle enlisted in the army air corps in the hope of becoming a pilot, but his poor hearing precluded this. Instead he was given an assignment as a radio operator and was stationed at Scott Air Force Base in Illinois (fig. 1.3). This assignment, however, aggravated his hearing problems, and he was made a member of a combat mapping unit and transferred to India. While there, he also worked as the army base librarian and was given the task of designing a temporary library—a first glimpse of the career that would await him.

In India during World War II Tuttle experienced new locales, new cultures, and new possibilities. This exposure would change the course of his life. He was struck by the simple dignity of the local people despite the hardships and deprivation they endured. His sensitivity to the human condition and to the vicissitudes of life was acute even at this early stage. His experiences reinforced a resolve to pursue his creative inclinations and to explore the expressive possibilities of applied design. Upon his return to Saint Louis following his discharge, he determined to become a designer of bridges. He later related that "They [bridges] are the most beautiful structural forms. And they have only one function: to carry traffic."[1] He was particularly enamored of the work of the early twentieth-century Swiss designer Robert Maillart and his principles of engineering reinforced concrete to create innovative bridge designs.[2] When he could not find an engineering program that taught Maillart's ideas or that involved hands-on experience, he sought out other avenues to the study of applied design.

Tuttle came to California in 1946 and used the GI Bill to enroll in the Art Center School in Los Angeles (now the Art Center College of Design in Pasadena). He was drawn to one of the school's most brilliant and influential teachers, Alvin Lustig, a Los Angeles-based designer who advocated a Bauhaus-inspired synthetic approach encompassing graphic, interior, and architectural design.[3] Although Lustig ultimately expelled Tuttle from the Art Center because he lacked formal training and had limited drafting skills, he was sufficiently taken with the young designer's intuitive talent to hire him on a part-time basis in his studio. Lustig's impact on Tuttle's design philosophy was significant and enduring, becoming a kind of mantra: "He taught me that if you analyzed a problem thoroughly enough, there is nothing that you can't do." According to Tuttle:

I was determined to hear what this man [Lustig] was about so I used to sit on the floor in the back of the class so no one could see me and listen to his lectures. And I did that, well not very long, I mean just three or four days, no more than that. He gave an assignment, and if I remember correctly it had to do with doing some sort of floating apparatus. You were living in a city, like New York, where you could open this thing up and hang your laundry on it to dry in a small space. So it all packs up, and you just slip it into the corner.

So I thought, well, I'm a fairly decent model maker—that's how I got by as well as I had anyhow—making models when I couldn't do other things. Anyway I made a model of this just as a challenge to myself. So I was sitting in the back of this class when they were making their presentations, and I thought, well shoot, there's no reason why I shouldn't get up and show mine, so I did. Well, man he had me out of there so fast you can't believe it. Al had quite a substantial ego. First of all, he didn't even know how I got in there in the first place, and neither did anybody else necessarily.... Anyway I made my little presentation, and he was furious. He absolutely exploded. And so out I went, out of the school.... but [in] maybe a week, two weeks, whatever it was, something like that, he made contact with me and wanted me to come in and work part-time a couple of days a week in his office. He wanted to see how my mind worked. I absolutely blew his mind. So we became quite close friends after this, and he was a strong influence.... I didn't learn anything about design from him other than the fact he was doing and preaching, you might say, what was abstractly in the back of my mind anyhow, and that is, "do not specialize." I mean after the war everything was specialization, and my whole life before was so narrow. So I thought I can't be pocketed this way ever again, and he taught me to think and...that if you analyze a problem thoroughly,... the very nature of the problem will lead you to a proper and appropriate solution. And that was my criterion from that point on.[4]

The Art Center School was but one context in which Tuttle was exposed to new ideas and approaches to design. The postwar years were a time of great experimentation in architecture and design, especially concerning the ways in which new technologies associated with industrial manufacturing could be applied to creative production, and Southern California had become a nexus of that activity. Tuttle knew and interacted with Charles Eames, George Nelson, Fred Usher, and others. He traveled to New York and worked briefly for Knoll Associates, helping to scout out and set up a new showroom. This work for Knoll took him back to Saint Louis briefly, and through his contacts there Tuttle learned about the Frank Lloyd Wright Fellowship at Taliesin West in Scottsdale, Arizona. Tuttle applied for and received the fellowship, spending five and a half months at Taliesin from 1948 to 1949: "It was an absolute phenomenon for me. I mean it shaped my life in many ways. Not because of the Wright routine but because of the desert and the way of life.... we lived in tents, the male members did; the women did not. And so we all had shepherds' tents, and I took my tent and did special things with it."[5]

This particular anecdote provides insight into Tuttle's independence and unique vision. Unlike his cohorts, who simply set up and used the tents given them, Tuttle altered his standard issue tent into a makeshift living space that responded to the surrounding environment. Wright took notice of "the special things" he had done and instead of chastising Tuttle for his departure (which was the expectation of his peers), Wright applauded him for his creativity and originality. After Tuttle left, Wright is said to have had a wood table made based on one of the designs Paul sketched while in residence, something Wright rarely did.[6]

From Taliesin, Tuttle returned to California, and after a brief stay in San Francisco, moved to the Los Angeles area in 1950. There he began designing showroom interiors for an Englishman named Arundel Clarke who had a shop of the same name on Melrose Place (fig. 1.5); Tuttle lived

1.4 Elliptical Coffee Table, 1950
Mahogany
Produced by Paul Tuttle,
Los Angeles, California
Collection of Laura Mullen

1.5 Showroom interior, c. 1950
Paul Tuttle, interior designer
Arundel Clarke store, Melrose Place,
Los Angeles, California

1.6 Armchair, 1950
Beech wood, cane
Produced by Paul Tuttle,
Los Angeles, California
Location unknown

in a small room off the showroom floor. Because Clarke distributed Knoll fabrics as well as hand-printed textiles by various artists, Tuttle met a number of local architects and designers who shopped there, including Thornton Ladd, who would have a major impact on Tuttle's early architectural career.

It was at this time that Tuttle designed and produced by hand his first pieces of furniture, based on advice he received from a retired cabinetmaker who happened to be his neighbor. His first coffee table (fig. 1.4), with its elegant elliptical top and gently tapered legs, was selected by Finn Juhl, the important mid-century Danish designer, for inclusion in the 1951 *Good Design* exhibition held at the Museum of Modern Art in New York and the Chicago Merchandise Mart. Charles Eames described the table as a successful adaptation of traditional craftsmanship to contemporary design.[7] The subtle play between the clean modernist lines of the solid mahogany top and the openwork leg configuration makes this simple table a sculptural statement. It introduces Tuttle's interest in exposing structure as a direct component in the conception of his furniture; it also reveals his fundamental preference for the warmth and sensuousness of wood. Moreover, despite its reference to mid-century Scandinavian design trends, this table subtly reveals Tuttle's proclivity for approaching things in a fresh way.

Tuttle's first chair (fig. 1.6), made of beech wood and cane (and known only through photographs), continued his preference for organic forms. The gentle curve of the arms and the adjustability of the back demonstrate that Tuttle was concerned with how the body makes contact with the chair. At the same time, the graceful flow of the lines of the beech-wood frame reveals his parallel concern with the aesthetic impact of furniture design. The chair was shown in 1951 at the Saint Louis Art Museum in the *Designer-Craftsman* exhibition, and its sensuous lines won Tuttle an award from the museum's Women's Board.

Although postwar Los Angeles provided a dynamic environment in terms of design, Tuttle chose to travel in Europe as a means of expanding his education. He made his first ocean crossing in 1952 and traveled widely on the continent. It was during this first trip that he met Finn Juhl in Denmark. There is little doubt about Tuttle's positive response to the Dane's sculptural approach to furniture design. This is especially evident in Tuttle's Armchair of 1952 (fig. 1.8a), which bears an uncanny resemblance to Juhl's Armchair of 1951 (fig. 1.7). Both reveal a tension between the linear composition of the walnut frame and the bold organic shapes of the upholstered seat and back. In Tuttle's version, however, there is an insistence on complicating the lines of the frame—especially the support structure for the seat—and the shape of the back to make a distinctive statement (fig 1.8b).

In the early 1950s, Tuttle produced a number of pieces for private residences that helped to crystallize his conception of furniture as either "organic," that is, designed to make contact with the human body, or "architectonic" and designed to exist structurally on its own:

An interesting facet in designing furniture is the scope or range one can travel. One can go from almost straight architectonic forms such as tables, to nearly organic sculpture such as chairs and direct contact pieces. Tables, work surfaces and cabinets all allow something leaning toward structure and a sense of that which is architectural. This is mainly because there is little direct physical contact. Chairs end up having an organic and sculptural feeling because we must usually make physical contact with them. Thereby they have much to do with human form and shape. Then there are all the ranges between these two opposite poles.[8]

1.7 Finn **Juhl** (1912–1989)
Armchair, 1951
Teak, leather
Baker Furniture, Grand Rapids, Michigan
Philadelphia Museum of Art:
Gift of Mr. and Mrs. N. Richard Miller,
1980, acc. no. 1980-138-1

1.8a, b Armchair, 1952
Walnut, metal, wool upholstery
Produced by John Van Breda,
Pasadena, California
Santa Barbara Museum of Art,
Gift of Barbara C. Wallace in memory
of Esther Bear and Mary O. Steel

1.9 Pedestal table and bench
by Paul Tuttle in the Ladd residence,
Pasadena, California, c. 1955

1.10 View of living room, Ladd residence,
Pasadena, California, c. 1955
Bench and pedestal tables by Paul Tuttle

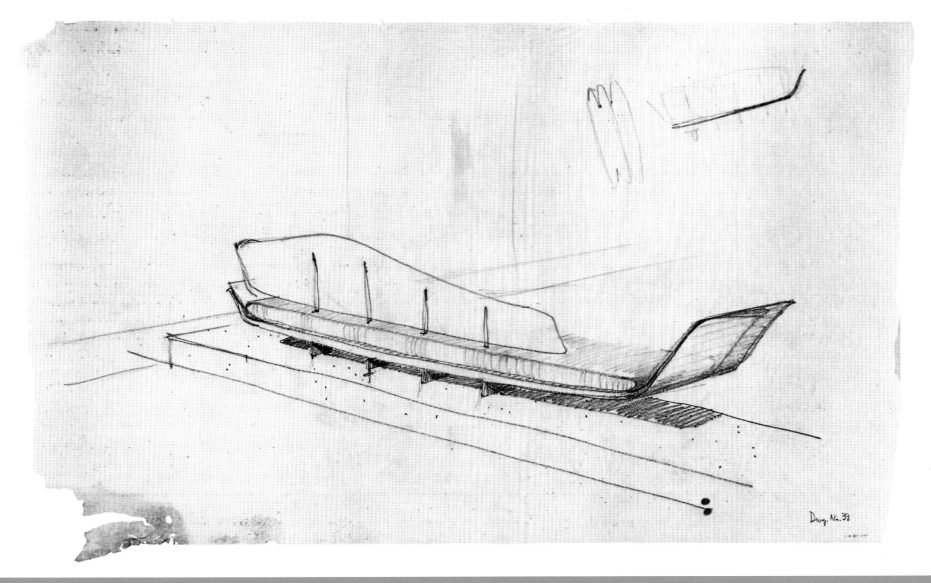

1.11 Bench sketch (Drawing 39), c. 1950
Pencil on paper
Collection of the University Art Museum,
UCSB, Architecture and Design Collection,
Gift of the artist

1.12 Vladimir **Kagan** (b. 1927)
Sofa, 1952

Because he lacked a formal education, one of Tuttle's strategies for expanding his knowledge base involved apprenticing with designers whom he respected, such as architects Welton Becket and Thornton Ladd. His time spent working with them in the mid-1950s mostly involved interior design projects. While working with Welton Becket, his primary assignment was the Joseph Magnin stores (see Kurt Helfrich's essay, chapter 3 of this volume.)

Indeed, many of Tuttle's early residential works were created for Thornton Ladd and Ladd's mother, Lillian. Tuttle did the interiors for the Ladd house and for the Ladd studio (both designed by Ladd); Tuttle lived in the studio until 1956. Among the most distinctive pieces he designed for Lillian Ladd were pedestal tables and benches that emphasized his attraction to organic forms. The small pedestal tables (fig. 1.9) were anchored to the floor from which they emerged like plants. Their simple, elegant forms make a natural reference to the famous pedestal tables of Eero Saarinen dating to the same year, which had freestanding cast aluminum bases. The bench he designed for Lillian Ladd, with its gracefully curved wood frame, is one of several he did during this early period, experimenting with form and line (fig. 1.10). Several drawings reveal his thought process, including one loosely sketched idea (fig. 1.11) illustrating his interest in exploring asymmetry and free-form shapes. This bench is clearly reminiscent of the biomorphism that characterized aspects of 1950s furniture design and is especially visible in the work of Isamu Noguchi and Vladimir Kagan (fig. 1.12).

Photographs of the Ladd studio (fig. 1.13) as Tuttle designed it during his residence clearly reveal his aesthetic, in which he sought to organically integrate the interior with the architecture and the landscape beyond. There is a striking horizontality to the architecture of the Ladd studio, emphasized by the flat overhanging roof and the cascading steps leading to the entry. Ladd designed the space as a kind of open, partitioned "cube" with wide expanses of window to minimize the boundary between the outside and the inside. Tuttle designed the interior of the sitting room (fig. 1.14) to reinforce this horizontality and made the focus of the room a central "floating" platform, which was carpeted in a celadon green. To the far left is an upholstered bench with adjustable sides and walnut legs; at the far right is his Armchair of 1952 (see figs. 1.8a, b). The low, glass-top coffee table is supported by a plank of wood that draws the eye down into the room. To add visual interest to an interior with furnishings that largely paralleled the floor plane, he made a slender sculptural construction out of wood and steel that projected vertically from the wood plank as if "coming out of a crack in the earth."

Similar in spirit but far grander in scale is the *Wind Harp*, the most dramatic sculptural work of Tuttle's career, produced in the early 1950s for the Ladd family property (figs. 1.15a, b). Thornton Ladd asked Tuttle to design a sculpture that would function as a strong vertical gesture. The result was a pair of twenty-one-foot-tall steel uprights, the shape of which echoes the designer's preference for the flow of a free-form line as well as his preoccupation with structure. As Thornton Ladd related, Tuttle had "the most exquisite sense of line of anybody I've ever seen with maybe the exception of the Japanese, or at least I think it's on a par with the Japanese. You know how they can just get a line and do a certain thing to it that makes it perfect? Paul had that ability."[9] The side view of the sculpture (fig. 1.15b) reveals the channeled cross-section of the rolled steel, which appears to be rigidly orthogonal in sharp contrast to the gentle curves of the frontal view. The verticality of this sculpture creates a striking visual counterpoint to the horizontal planes of the house and garden. The steel was painted Tyrian, a dark black-purple, to give it added formal distinction.

1.13 Exterior view, Ladd studio,
Pasadena, California, c. 1954
Thornton Ladd, architect,
with Paul Tuttle, interior designer

1.14 Interior, Ladd studio,
Pasadena, California, c. 1954
Thornton Ladd, architect,
with Paul Tuttle, interior designer

1.15a, b Wind Harp,
outside Ladd residence,
Pasadena, California, c. 1950
Produced by Walter Lacy, Jr.

1.16a, b Adjustable Table, 1962
Walnut, metal
Produced by Stanley Reifel, Carpinteria, California
Collection of the University Art Museum, UCSB,
Purchase by Friends of Paul Tuttle Fund

Although this outdoor sculpture is site specific and reflects Tuttle's consistent focus on structure, it also exposes a side of his creativity that has long made his work aesthetically compelling as well as functionally appropriate. He spent a lifetime struggling with the tension between the needs of applied design and the greater freedom that purely artistic expression offers:

You know, I think that I feel very strongly that there's a certain force outside of myself that works through me. I mean, I really have allowed myself to be vulnerable enough to let certain things come out which have not been my inherited nature. In other words, I'm a constructionist. A constructionist is where you are conscious of how structure works—you can't do a sculpture in the real sense of it and have structure at a conscious level take over. [To be pure sculpture] there has to be a certain abandonment that destroys that very thing.[10]

Tuttle moved to Santa Barbara, California, in 1956 and began his professional life as a freelance designer. He continued to live there until his death in 2002. In the late 1950s and early 1960s he experimented broadly with forms and materials, designing a variety of seating and tables that were fabricated by the Santa Barbara-area craftsman Stanley Reifel. One of his most distinctive designs of this period is a walnut Adjustable Table (1962; figs. 1.16a, b), the top of which can be lowered to accommodate a chair for reading or writing or raised to function as a wall table. The central slant board is also adjustable according to the intended function of the table. This piece initiated an exploration of multipurpose tables. The five height adjustments for the table are made by means of a simple metal rod; later in his career Tuttle adapted simple but ingenious mechanisms, such as a bicycle sprocket, for raising or lowering the height (see fig. 1.73). The detailing of the Adjustable Table of 1962, especially the treatment of the legs, imparts a lightness and grace.

Another table from this period exemplifies Tuttle's structural playfulness, manifest above all in furniture that could function equally well as sculpture. His Spiral Table (1964; fig. 1.17) was originally designed for a private residence but was later selected by Gere Kavanaugh, a Los Angeles-based designer, for use in dressing rooms at the Joseph Magnin's stores. Fabricated of thin rods of wrought iron, the table base traces a delicate spiral. Tuttle referred to its whimsical form as "a piece of joy."

The number of distinctive chair designs that Tuttle created in these early years supports his claim that they are "the greatest design challenge." Several demonstrate his fascination with the tension between form and structure, line and mass. The Pony Chair (1961; figs. 1.18a, b) has a complexity of line and detail that expresses its handcrafted sculptural quality and prevents it from being straightforward or conventional. Tuttle's "exquisite line" begins with the front legs and continues to the arms and back rail. The chair's name refers to the way in which the delicately "bowed" legs resemble the "uncertain, wobbly legs of a pony."[11] The exposed bolts and pegs in the chair's construction reveal a loving attention to detail and the combination of lustrous walnut with cane and sheepskin make this chair comfortable as well as elegant.

From this same period, the Dining Chair of 1959 (see fig. 2.7) shows a related conceptualization of a chair's essential structure and introduces the designer's career-long exploration of the tension in legs that gently flare outward to achieve a delicacy of line while maintaining sufficient strength to support the weight of a sitter. The "lightness" of this early chair frame led to a series of seating with similarly flaring legs that join at the top in an inverted "Y" formation. The first Inverted "Y" Lounge Chair of 1960 (fig. 1.19) asserts the strength of this formation through lamination and the low and wide branching of the legs.

1.17 Spiral Table, 1964
Wrought iron, glass
Produced by Walter Cardaro,
Santa Barbara, California
Private Collection

1.18a, b Pony Chair, 1961
Walnut, cane, sheepskin
Produced by Stanley Reifel,
Carpinteria, California
Collection of Georgia and Ted Funsten

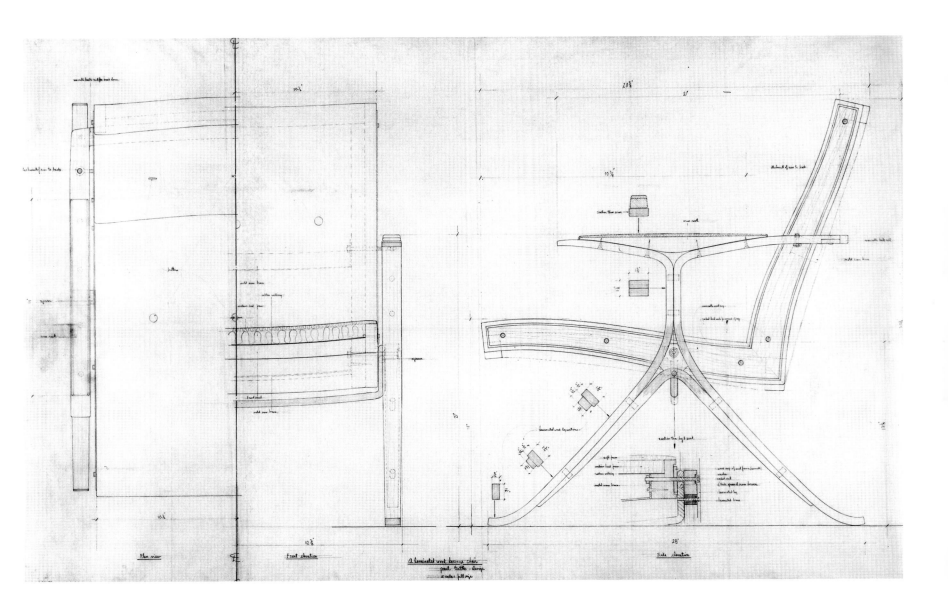

1.19 Inverted "Y" Lounge Chair, 1960
Walnut, leather (reupholstered)
Produced by Stanley Reifel,
Carpinteria, California
Collection of Alma and Paul Gray

1.20 Inverted "Y" Lounge Chair,
plan, elevation, and section, 1960
Pencil on paper
Collection of the University Art Museum,
UCSB, Architecture and Design Collection,
Gift of the artist

The rare existing drawing of this chair shows how Tuttle carefully worked out the details in material, structure, and construction (fig. 1.20).

In 1966 Tuttle launched the related "66" Series, where steel was added to strengthen the chair's structure and to function in ways that wood could not (fig. 1.21). The U-shaped steel brace under the seat was an important structural addition; it also provided a key design element. According to Tuttle: "A little bit of metal is like jewelry on a woman. It makes a distinct difference."[12] The evolution of this chair preoccupied Tuttle until he felt he had achieved a final resolution of its design in 1995 (see fig 1.98).

Tuttle's interest in structure also led him to explore the adaptation of certain architectural principles to furniture. His series of Little Dining Chairs in the early 1960s was based on simple post-and-beam construction (fig. 1.22). Their handcrafted sturdiness and traditional design are reminiscent of mid-century Scandinavian work, especially Hans Wegner's popular Round Chair of 1949 (see fig. 2.30). However, the complexity and freshness of the design, evident in the articulation of the back rail and its connection to the arms, make these chairs uniquely "Tuttle."

An even greater debt to architecture is evident in Tuttle's most important and now-famous chair from these early years, the prototype "Z" Chair of 1964 (fig. 1.23). Originally named the "Rocket Launcher" by Tuttle, because of its sense of movement and spring, this is among the most effective and elegant adaptations of the architectural cantilever to the chair. "Every engineer who saw my sketch defied me on this. But I knew from the kinds of loads the cantilever supports in architecture that it could certainly carry a person, as long as the materials were strong enough."[13] The use of steel allowed Tuttle to achieve something that was completely impossible in wood:

On the original "Z" Chair that cantilever, that is a son of a gun, and it takes all the weight on the end of it. But I never had any question about that really holding up. Again, the quality of the weld is there because I had worked it…. The crazy cantilevers in buildings, which were carrying enormous amounts of weight in the steel structure, gave me an insight into what I felt you could achieve with steel [in furniture] that I couldn't achieve with wood, since I am a wood lover basically. And it really excited me enormously, since I gave a preference to wood. Yet I was in a certain way forced into using metal to explore these things, then almost immediately I said, "Well, I'm going to challenge it to the limit." This was my excitement in it. And I did it the best I could in a purely intuitive way.[14]

In 1966 Tuttle was given the Carson Pirie Scott Young Designer Award for the originality and freshness of the "Z" Chair design. The name that the chair acquired, loosely based on the gestural form of the spring steel, originated with Tuttle's initial humorous reference to it as "zee" chair:

Well, as I told you, the original "Z" Chair was never intended to be called a "Z" Chair. I was trying to be funny with "The Chair," so I said, "Zee Chair." But it stuck with it. It's like you get stuck with a nickname. And so, over time as the chair developed, more and more I came to the conclusion I had to find some way to justify the name. So it really became a "Z" Chair.[15]

The first "Z" Chair was shown in the *California Design*/9 exhibition of 1965 at the Pasadena Art Museum. In the spirit of the early 1950s *Good Design* exhibitions held in New York and Chicago, this triennial juried show of objects made in California was intended to display the "latest implements of living"—the best in industrial design, furniture, and crafts, from handmade one-of-a-kind works of art to objects able to meet the rigors of mass production. *California*

1.21 "66" Chair, 1966
Walnut, steel, faux leopard
Produced by Stanley Reifel,
Carpinteria, California
Collection of Valerie and Scott Youmans

1.22 Little Dining Chair, 1963
Walnut, cane
Produced by Stanley Reifel,
Carpinteria, California
Collection of Mr. and Mrs. Edgar B. Ward

Design/8 in 1962 had also featured several pieces that Tuttle had designed in the late 1950s and early 1960s.[16]

Eudorah Moore, the curator of design at the Pasadena Art Museum, was both juror and director of the *California Design* exhibition program. She also was one of the judges who selected Paul Tuttle as "California designer of the year," when he received the Carson Pirie Scott Young Designer Award for his "Z" Chair. She had met Tuttle when he lived in the Ladd studio, as she and her husband were his neighbors. In late 1966 Moore organized a month-long "retrospective" exhibition, *The Furniture Designs of Paul Tuttle*, featuring key works from the 1950s and 1960s beginning with his Elliptical Coffee Table of 1950 (see fig. 1.4). Tuttle also designed the installation, which was as original as his furniture, and used lengths of chain-mail fencing hung ceiling to floor to divide the space into separate areas.[17] The accompanying illustrated catalog opened with a statement by Moore, which is as true today as it was then:

The designs of Paul Tuttle, whether they be a house, a chair or a bottle, are each a sculpture for use. Always simple but never stark, within a wide framework of linear expression, they invite touch, delight the eye. Each design stands as a statement on its own merit. A cerebrated solution, slowly and painstakingly evolved, emerges finally with a pristine quality, never trite, never an adapted statement. Yet, emerging from a mind sensitive to human needs and responsive to the human element, it can be invested with tactile pleasure, visual excitement and even humor. Paul Tuttle stands among the top designers of furniture today by virtue of his uncompromising integrity, his response to materials, and by his talent for drawing the best from the past and the present to make a very personal design statement for our time.[18]

At this juncture Tuttle had received considerable attention in Southern California for his design work. Not only was he much in the press because of the Pasadena *California Design* exhibitions and his own furniture retrospective but also because of his innovative work in architectural design, which he undertook in Santa Barbara between 1959 and 1967.[19] Tuttle was particularly influenced by Thornton Ladd's work, especially Ladd's design for his own studio, which Tuttle considered "the most beautiful small piece of architecture I've ever seen."[20]

Tuttle applied his fascination with structure to the design for a beach house in Carpinteria (1959) commissioned by Mary Lou and George Dangerfield (fig. 1.24; see also figs. 3.12, 3.13). His structural fascination is especially evident in the way the columns of the house cantilever out of the piers, providing sufficient lateral strength for construction in an earthquake zone, and a clerestory window that makes the roof appear to float. It is likely that the experience of Ladd's small open studio with its clear integration of interior and exterior provided the inspiration for this house. Writing about Tuttle's "Beach Pavilion" in 1961, the architecture critic Henry J. Seldis noted that "The open aspect of the small beach house provides it with a sense of spaciousness and light. The interior is closely linked with the beach and plants around it, yet its working and living areas provide intimacy and quietude rarely found on a beach."[21]

The structural distinctiveness of this beach house, which became its hallmark, was in part Tuttle's response to the lifestyle of his clients. He had met the Dangerfields soon after he arrived in Santa Barbara through local gallery owner Esther Bear. Mary Lou Dangerfield was so taken with the photographs Tuttle showed her of the tent he had transformed at Taliesin West that she asked him to design the beach house.[22] A few years later he also designed

1.23 "Z" Chair (prototype), 1964
Chrome-plated steel, leather
Produced by Carson-Johnson, Inc.,
Los Angeles, California
Collection of Joan and Jim Tanner

1.24 Dangerfield Beach House, c. 1961
Paul Tuttle, designer, with Lawrence Harlow, architect

1.25 Tuttle residence, 1961–1962
Paul Tuttle, designer, with Robert Garland, architect

a primary residence for the Dangerfields high in the canyon above their beach house in Carpinteria. Because of their desire for privacy (especially after the attention the beach house attracted), few photographs exist of this residence (see fig. 3.15). Something of the magic it held for its owners is, however, evident in this letter from George Dangerfield, a Pulitzer-prize winning historian, written to Tuttle while the designer was in Europe in 1961:

I meant to write to you before, but I am not really a letter-writer, just as some people are not swimmers or acrobats; and I am only taking the plunge now or lurching off the trapeze, or whatever, because I feel absolutely impelled to say something to you before you leave Europe. It's about yourself and also about us—and it is simply that even you, with all your imagination and sympathy, might find it difficult to believe what a joy this house is becoming. Of course "becoming": because all truth, and this house is true, grows towards itself. I knew it was good from the very beginning, but my experience of it has equally of course been like waking up very early in the morning and watching the light grow. And though we did from the beginning go over and over the plans, so that the house was from its inception a mutual experience, what I see growing is your central vision, which you have been good enough to share with us, and which we share with you. Your vision of what a house on this hill and beneath these mountains ought to be and must be has been justified and is being fulfilled: there are times when I and Mary Lou experience a pleasure more pure and piercing than any-thing we ever supposed an environment could give us. That is what I want to tell you while you are in Europe.[23]

As an outgrowth of Tuttle's close friendship with the Dangerfields, he designed a small house for himself adjacent to theirs on Toro Canyon Road in 1961–1962 (fig 1.25). They shared a car park, but otherwise the two houses could not be more different in scale or in spirit. Tuttle's was designed to function as his studio and residence, and it clearly reflects his preference for small-scale spaces and a pure sculptural spareness. Drawing on Greek ver-nacular houses, his was essentially a small "box" anchored to its site by a long white wall.[24] The north-south orienta-tion took full advantage of ocean and mountain views, and the interior, essentially one large room with a deeply recessed terrace, extended the living space outward to the canyon beyond. The tall cypress trees he planted provide a striking visual counterpoint to the horizontal sweep of the house and wall, echoing the way the dramatic verti-cality of his *Wind Harp* relieved the Ladd property of its predominant horizontality. This was Tuttle's most distinctive and personal architectural statement—truly integrating the architecture with the environment. The house has been deservedly and frequently reviewed and acclaimed over the years.[25]

THE SWISS YEARS

In 1958 Tuttle launched a parallel career in Switzerland, beginning as a corporate design consultant to the Basel-based pharmaceutical firm of Doetsch, Grether & Cie. Tuttle had met Hans Grether in 1957 through Thornton Ladd and a mutual friend in Pasadena. Grether saw what Tuttle had done in the Ladd studio and the next year invited him to come to Switzerland to design a conference room in the company's headquarters in Basel. This first commission ultimately led to the total design of the building's sixth floor, which included a main conference room with sectional tables that could seat up to twenty-six. An early photograph of this space (fig. 1.29) shows the main sections of the conference table, which seat eighteen, along with the conference chairs, a version of Tuttle's Armchair of 1952 upholstered in leather (see figs. 1.8a, b). Tuttle designed everything in the space, including the cabinetry for storage and display and the recessed display area

1.26 Paul Tuttle in Switzerland in the early 1970s.

1.27 Tuttle bought this Volkswagen dune buggy in Switzerland in the early 1970s because he loved its design and its simple construction.

1.28 Paul Tuttle with Hans
and Esther Grether in their
dining nook, 1963–1964
Doetsch, Grether & Cie.
Headquarters, Basel, Switzerland

in an adjoining wall. Grether was an art collector and his collection featured important Chinese ceramics and other early Tang Dynasty pieces, as well as works by such European modernists as Giacometti, Chagall, Klee, and Ernst. Tuttle designed pedestals and wall units to showcase the collection. He also designed a small dining nook for the space with two black leather couch/seats that flank a table cantilevered off the wall and supported by a single openwork pedestal (fig. 1.28). All these pieces share the clean, modernist sensibility of Tuttle's early work, with a focus on the harmonious combination of warm walnut and rich black leather. With their simple elegance and purity of materials, they have stood the test of time and look as much at home in Esther Grether's new residence as they did in the 1960s.[26]

After completing this first project, Tuttle continued to spend several months per year in Europe, initially working on various projects commissioned by Hans Grether and other corporate clients in Basel, such as Dreyfus Bank. He designed three additional conference rooms for the Doetsch, Grether & Cie. headquarters, including a small meeting room favored by company employees because of its intimacy. Designed in the early 1960s, this room features a circular pedestal table made of walnut that is anchored to the floor (fig. 1.32). In the early 1980s he designed the largest of the firm's conference rooms, which included a flexible configuration of tables that could seat a variable number of staff and clients (figs.1.30, 1.31).[27] The long, rectilinear, maple and Formica table is constructed in two sections. An Italian bicycle wheel supports each end and allows the table to be moved easily. The curved ends of the table make it possible for it to join a second circular table for maximum seating. Although these tables clearly relate to other custom work Tuttle was doing in the 1980s in Santa Barbara, his design decisions were driven by the way the furniture would actually be used by Doetsch, Grether staff:

I did the pyramid base on the round table because I wanted to put an emphasis on the merchandise which would be placed in the center of it, in the glass area.... The base is a five-sided pyramid because the table top is actually done in five sections. The [pyramid gives] substance to the table because of its dimensions.... The other conference table is in this elongated diamond shape so that people will have a sense of communication. It is a table that will seat sixteen, eighteen, or twenty people.[28]

Tuttle used the experience of being abroad for part of each year as a dynamic learning laboratory:

Europe is my education. Europe allows me my objectivity. It is not where the design comes from. Doetsch, Grether first tried for two to three years to get me to live there on a permanent retainer to be at their disposal. I turned them down. I mean, California has to do with creating. Europe for me, since I'm not educated, is an education... it does not have to do with my designing here.... those first years I worked with Doetsch, Grether, every single weekend I went to Paris or somewhere in France or to Florence, or some place, visiting cathedrals and churches and eleventh-, twelfth-, thirteenth-, and fifteenth-century architecture. And if I would have become an expatriate, I would have probably within two to three years hardly been designing any longer, just studying.[29]

It was through the connections Paul Tuttle had made while working in Basel for Doetsch, Grether & Cie. that he was introduced to Alex Strässle in 1967.[30] Strässle International was founded in 1886 with the goal of producing furniture combining function with artistic and technically innovative design for residential and contract markets. In 1955 the company began hiring internationally recognized architects to design new furniture. Tuttle was suggested to Alex Strässle on the basis of his innovative design work in Switzerland and in California. Alex invited Paul to visit

1.29 (Opposite)
Conference room, c. 1960
Doetsch, Grether & Cie. Headquarters,
Basel, Switzerland
Paul Tuttle, interior designer

1.30 (Top, left)
Conference room, c. 1980
Doetsch, Grether & Cie. Headquarters,
Basel, Switzerland
Paul Tuttle, interior designer

1.31 (Top, right)
Conference room, c. 1980
Doetsch, Grether & Cie. Headquarters,
Basel, Switzerland
Paul Tuttle, interior designer

1.32 (Bottom)
Conference room, c. 1960
Doetsch, Grether & Cie. Headquarters,
Basel, Switzerland
Paul Tuttle, interior designer

the Strässle collection and factory in Kirchberg, Switzerland. Tuttle showed Alex and Maria Strässle drawings of his furniture designs, including the "Z" Chair, which had just garnered so many honors in California. Maria remembers Paul's first visit to their home in Kirchberg and her impressions of him thus:

Alex announced to me there was a designer who was suggested by a friend in Basel. I was just preparing lunch and pregnant, and so Paul arrived. An extraordinary little man. I couldn't believe that such a man had come to our house, and he showed us the designs, and I was absolutely surprised. I never saw such a thing because I had always dealt with designers but not ones with such lines, and so I was, at that moment really surprised and astonished and glad to have another face before me.... For myself, I felt, "Yes, we should do something with Paul."[31]

Tuttle entered into a contractual agreement with Strässle International in 1968 that allowed him to spend six months a year working in Switzerland, which he did until 1983 (figs. 1.26, 1.27). Except for a few commissions in Santa Barbara, nearly all the work he did in those years was for Strässle International or for private Swiss clients. Between 1968 and 1973 Strässle produced seventeen of Tuttle's designs, some of which were furniture lines that included coordinated seating and tables. Several of these pieces have become Strässle classics and are still in production today. Because of the company's reliance on new developments in contemporary European design, especially from Italy, much of what Tuttle created for Strässle recalled the cooly geometric metal, leather, and glass furnishings that have been identified under the rubric "International Modernism."[32]

Tuttle's first design for production was a reworking of his "Z" Chair of 1964, which became the centerpiece of Strässle's

Zeta series (fig. 1.34). Although the elegant lines of the chrome-plated strap steel have been retained (with bolts used to join the pieces rather than the more delicate welding possible in the custom version), the Zeta Lounge Chair (fig. 1.33) is somewhat wider and higher than the original and has denser upholstery. One of the hallmarks of Strässle furniture is its beautiful leather upholstery, and many of the pieces Tuttle designed for the firm take advantage of this. A two-seat lounge, tables, and a dining/conference chair were also produced as part of the Zeta Series (see fig. 1.63a), but a striking bench design exists only in prototype (fig. 1.36). It shows Tuttle's adaptation of his earlier design in wood (see fig. 1.10) to the clean lines and strength of bent spring steel.

The Symbol Chair of 1969 (fig. 1.35) was an interesting development out of the Zeta Chair. It relies on the cantilever of the latter but uses chrome-plated tubular steel with a continuous loop to support the seat and back. Although the natural spring in the frame provided comfortable seating, problems arose in the welding of the steel parts. Some of Tuttle's designs could not go into production because technical and structural complexities of this sort could not be resolved in an economically feasible manner.

The early years with Strässle offered Tuttle the opportunity to test new materials. Experimentation with synthetics was characteristic of 1960s furniture design, and Tuttle took advantage of the company's production capabilities as well as Alex Strässle's interest in innovation. Starting in 1969 Tuttle designed several experimental pieces. The first was the Apollo Lounge Chair (fig. 1.37), which had a large polyurethane foam shell and leather upholstery. Over the next few years he designed another lounge chair with a molded thermoplastic shell, the Alfa (1972; fig. 1.38), which was the largest of its type to be produced at that time.[33] Strässle produced as well the fiberglass conference

1.34 (Opposite)
Promotional shot of Tuttle's designs
for the Zeta series produced
by Strässle International, Switzerland

1.35 (Top)
Symbol Chair, 1969
Chrome-plated steel, leather
Produced by Strässle International,
Switzerland

1.36 (Bottom)
Zeta Bench (prototype), c. 1968
Chrome-plated strap steel, leather
Produced by Strässle International,
Switzerland

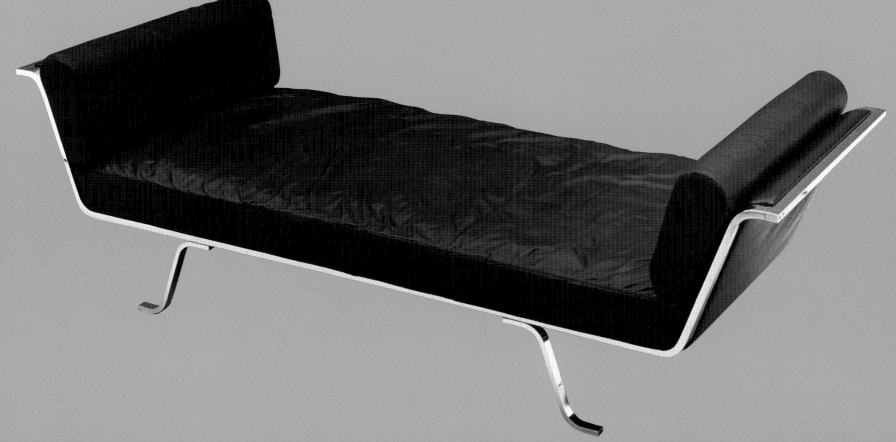

chair with leather upholstery and a chrome-plated strap steel base that Tuttle designed especially for Doetsch, Grether to use in one of its conference rooms (fig. 1.39). A line of sectional fiberglass seating and tables (fig. 1.40) and a molded plastic lamp in both a table top and standing version (see p. 188) were also produced by Strässle from Tuttle's designs. The standing Crane Lamp, as Tuttle called it, was seven feet tall and had a five-foot adjustable arm from which the molded lamp shade was suspended. The delicate wire armature minimized the lamp's mass and created an elegant foil to the simple hemispherical white plastic shade. Only a few of these striking lamps were produced.

One of the most successful pieces involving the use of new plastic materials that Tuttle did with Strässle was a stacking chair, called the PT 200, which had a molded polypropylene seat and back with a tubular steel base (fig. 1.41). Several versions were produced at different heights with various base configurations; the shell was offered in a range of colors. The most elegant version features L-shaped legs, achieving the spareness of design Tuttle preferred. Subtle indentations in the chair's seat allowed it to be easily stacked and loaded onto a dolly. These chairs enjoyed great popularity on the European market, competing with the famous Eames Fiberglass Stacking Chair of 1955. Unlike the Eames version, however, Tuttle's chairs were meant to be freestanding (fig. 1.42) and not linked in horizontal rows. Speaking of his experimentation with this chair, Tuttle recalled

There are some lines that happened with that chair which are very, very nice.... And, the little detail that locks the thing in so when you stack them, they really stay stacked. All those things really did work on that little chair...it was the only piece of any of the molded things that ever had

what should have been there.... It brought out more of my kind of thinking—form in relationship to the body.[34]

The last experimental synthetic pieces that Tuttle designed for Strässle were and continue to be the most successful commercially. The Leonardo Collection, comprising variations on a single chair type (figs. 1.43, 1.44), has been popular because it combines very innovative materials with a strongly traditional form. The style of the Leonardo has been said to resemble a nineteenth-century Windsor Chair, and the back rail has the simple lines of Scandinavian modern chairs, especially recalling Hans Wegner's Round, or Classic, Chair (see fig. 2.30).[35] At the same time, its form continues Tuttle's exploration of post-and-beam structural principles, following the stylistic model of his Little Dining Chair (see fig. 1.22).

The innovation in the Leonardo (named after the great da Vinci) lay in the development of a self-skinning polyurethane foam, which formed the contoured seat and back rail. Tuttle carved the original pieces out of wood, and from the wood a steel-reinforced fiberglass mold was created for production.[36] The injected polyurethane foam results in a tough outer skin and a soft core when removed from the mold. Heavy elephant hide was used to create the mold's "bumpy" outer texture (resembling leather and resisting slipping), and the finished black, "self-skinned" surface is washable and comfortable. The chair knocked down for shipping and came with plain or dyed beech wood or steel legs that were bolted in place. The Leonardo has met with particularly strong commercial success in Japan, especially for a contract furniture market. The High Stool version of the Leonardo (fig. 1.43) was selected for inclusion in the important exhibition held at the Smithsonian Institution in 1981 titled *Innovative Furniture in America from 1800 to the Present*.[37]

1.37 Apollo Lounge Chair, 1969
Polyurethane, leather, steel
Produced by Strässle International,
Switzerland

1.38 Alfa Lounge Chair, 1972
Thermoplastic, upholstery, steel
Produced by Strässle International,
Switzerland

1.39 Conference Chair, 1973
Fiberglass, leather, steel
Produced by Strässle International,
Switzerland

1.40 Couch, 1969
Fiberglass, foam, upholstery
Produced by Strässle International,
Switzerland

1.41 PT 200 Stacking Chairs, 1969
Steel tubing, polypropylene
Produced by Strässle International, Switzerland
Collection of the University Art Museum,
UCSB, Architecture and Design Collection,
Gift of Maria and Alex Strässle

1.42 PT 200s in Municipal Theater,
Saint Gall, Switzerland
Promotional image

1.43 Leonardo High Stool, 1979
Promotional image

1.44 Leonardo Chair (variation), 1979
Self-skinning polyurethane, steel, painted beech
Produced by Strässle International, Switzerland
Collection of the University Art Museum,
UCSB, Architecture and Design Collection,
Gift of Maria and Alex Strässle

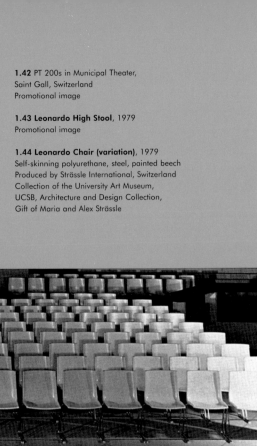

Despite this groundbreaking work, the most striking outcome of Tuttle's tenure as a contract designer for Strässle was his exploration of the structural and aesthetic possibilities of designing with tubular and strap steel (fig. 1.45). Steel provided the strength he needed to create furniture with clean pure minimalist lines, and it was highly adaptable to industrial production. His work in this medium owes a debt to the modern designs of such Bauhaus visionaries as Marcel Breuer, Mies van der Rohe, Le Corbusier, and Mart Stam, whose tubular steel chairs of the 1920s and 1930s epitomized the motto "form follows function."[38] This philosophy and the aesthetic that grew out of it are central to Tuttle's thinking and were expressed creatively in much of the work he did for Strässle. His first design, the Circle Chair (1970; fig 1.48), is a complex arrangement of intersecting bends of tubular steel with a full circle anchoring the base. The seat and back are made of heavy leather designed like a sling. These back and seat elements are joined by a belt buckle that would normally be used to attach a cowbell—an object with which Tuttle had become enamored during his sojourns in the Swiss countryside.

In the 1970s he designed two other leather and steel furniture lines for Strässle that proved very successful on the contract market. The first includes a conference/dining chair, an armchair, and a conference table, called the Celina Series (named for one of the Strässle daughters). It is notable for its comfort and simplicity of design (fig. 1.49). More distinctive from a design point of view is the second, Tuttle's Anaconda Series of 1970/1971 (fig. 1.47). The three-legged chair makes a bold sweeping gesture in the continuous line of the front legs and backrest. A single back leg joins this element and forms an upside down "T" at the ground. Tuttle's prototype for the chair (fig. 1.46) allowed this strong linear composition to dominate, providing no padding for the back support other than a minimal wrapping with leather. Since the need for comfort

prevailed, especially given the chair's use for dining and office seating, a curved upholstered form was added to the back but with a strategic opening to reveal the chair's structure. As an accompaniment Tuttle created the Anaconda Table, otherwise known as the "Fat Tube" Table, out of a dramatic swirl of wide tubular steel (fig.1. 50). It was designed, in part, as a response to the characterization of his earlier wood pieces as "fragile." The generous muscularity of the "Fat Tube" table makes it one of the most unusual designs in the Strässle corpus.

Combining the cool, jewel-like luster of chromed steel with the rich softness of leather upholstery are three other pieces that are unequivocally Tuttle's most distinctive and best-selling designs for Strässle: the Chariot Chaise (1972; fig. 1.51), the Nonna Rocking Chair (1972; fig. 1.53), and the Arco Chair (1976; fig. 1.54). The Chariot is the first of several chaise longues that Tuttle designed over the course of his career. The chaise presents an interesting design challenge as the "longue" component needs to relate organically to the body and then be held in a stationary position with a compatible structural support. Many of the early lounge designs by such eminent designers as Mies (1931) and Le Corbusier (1928; fig. 1.52) used a bent tubular steel frame to support the upholstered and ergonomically complex reclining surface in much the same way that Tuttle did. However, the rigid structure of the base, especially in the famous example by Le Corbusier, takes away from the fluidity of the tubular steel lines. Tuttle relaxed the curves of the reclining surface and used one fluid sweep of tubular steel to support the base. Although it lacked the extreme spareness of Scandinavian designer Paul Kjaerholm's Hammock of 1965, Tuttle's Chariot has a refined elegance that has made it a very popular seller for Strässle. The pieced leather upholstery adds visual interest and textural contrast while providing comfort for the user.

1.45 **Toro Lounge Chair**, 1971
Promotional image

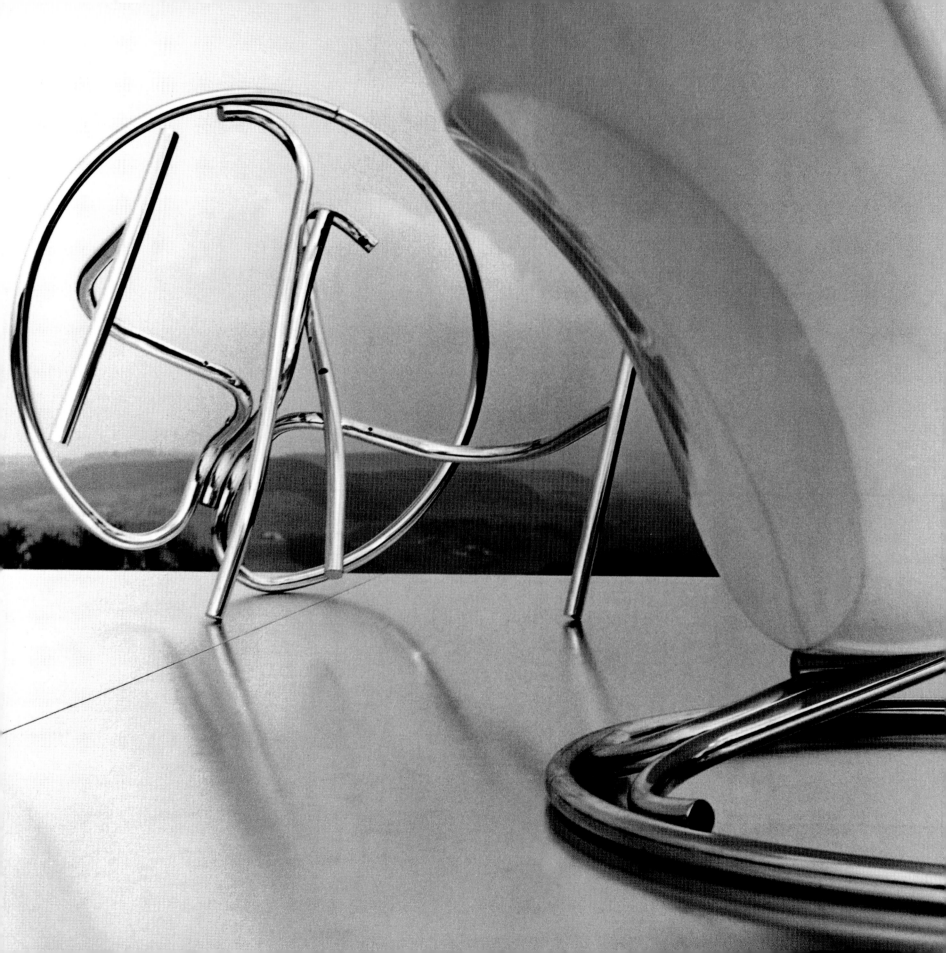

1.46 Anaconda Chair (prototype), 1970
Chrome-plated tubular steel, leather
Produced by Strässle International, Switzerland

1.47 Anaconda Chair (Three-legged), 1970/1971
Chrome-plated tubular steel, leather
Produced by Strässle International, Switzerland
Collection of Candice and Farshid Assassi

1.48 Circle Chair, 1970
Chrome-plated tubular steel, leather
Produced by Strässle International, Switzerland
Collection of Carol and Fred Kenyon

1.49 Celina Chair and Celina Conference Table, 1970
Chrome-plated tubular steel
and leather; tubular steel, maple
Produced by Strässle International, Switzerland

1.50 Anaconda Table (Fat Tube Table), 1970/1971
Chrome-plated tubular steel, glass
Produced by Strässle International, Switzerland
Collection of Robert and Mary Looker

1.51 (Top) **Chariot Chaise**, 1972
Chrome-plated tubular steel, leather
Produced by Strässle International, Switzerland
Collection of the University Art Museum,
UCSB, Architecture and Design Collection,
Gift of the artist

1.52 (Bottom), **Le Corbusier** (1887–1965),
Pierre **Jeanneret** (1896–1967),
Charlotte **Perriand** (b. 1903)
Chaise Longue à reglage, 1928
Chrome-plated tubular steel, painted wood, fabric
Produced by Thonet Frères, Paris
Vitra Design Museum, Weil am Rhein

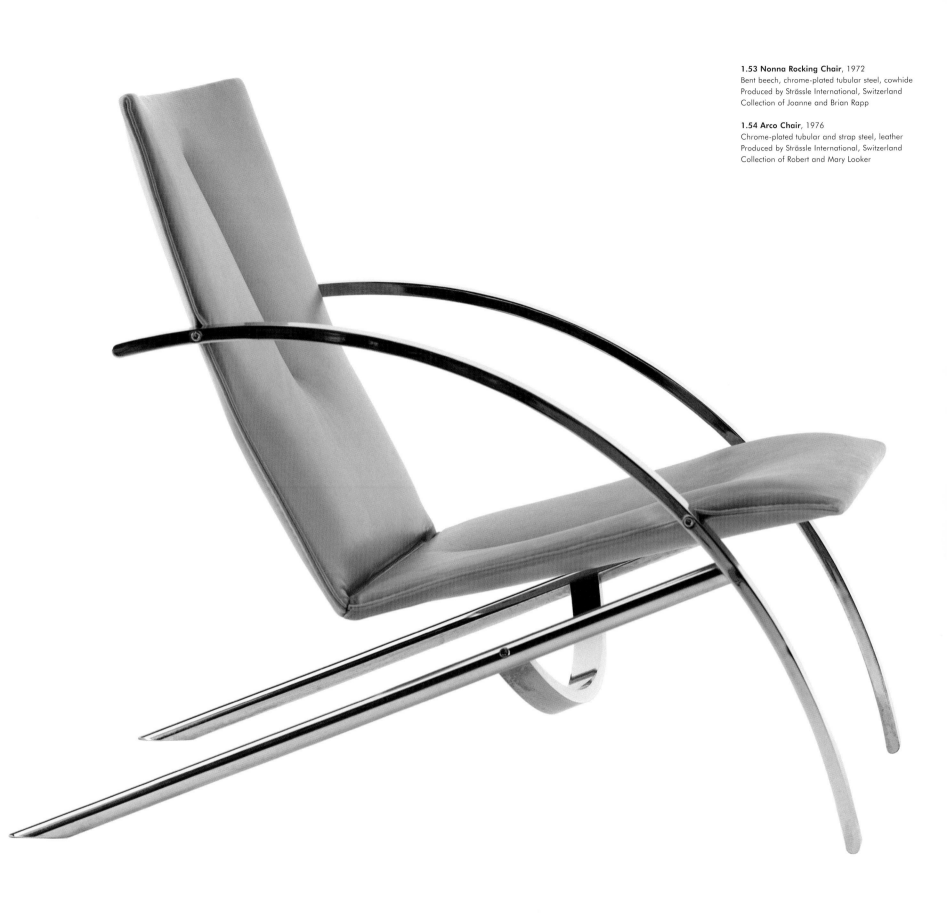

1.53 Nonna Rocking Chair, 1972
Bent beech, chrome-plated tubular steel, cowhide
Produced by Strässle International, Switzerland
Collection of Joanne and Brian Rapp

1.54 Arco Chair, 1976
Chrome-plated tubular and strap steel, leather
Produced by Strässle International, Switzerland
Collection of Robert and Mary Looker

The Nonna (Italian for "grandmother") Rocking Chair is Tuttle's response to the Thonet classic—the design of which he admired, although he found the chair uncomfortable to sit in. Guido Baumgartner, vice president of Thonet America, challenged Tuttle to design a more comfortable bentwood rocker. As Tuttle remembered:

Guido Baumgartner was coming here [to Kirchberg] with the intent of getting a collection of my pieces which would be handled by Thonet of America. In conversation one day after lunch, I said how much I liked the original Thonet rocker, but it really wasn't very comfortable. And he said, "Well then, why don't you do one that is?"

I thought for a minute, and I said, "Okay, I will." And that was the end of that. I went to work on the idea of doing a Thonet rocker that would be comfortable. And I wanted to get bentwood into it, but I remembered in the old rocker, in the rocking part of it, that the wood was the part that got the real movement, and it would loosen up. And so I did the combination of the wood and metal. And I wanted an area for the arms to have some chance of resting.... And then, Alex [Strässle] wanted to do a sling because that was a simple thing for Strässle to do; they can do it just with a flat pattern. One part reinforces the seat so that it doesn't have as much give; it is then doubled under the knees. The piece across the back supports the small of the back, and the more it shapes to the body, the more the support is the significant part of it.... And then, I designed the rocker in such a way that the wood piece is slightly above the metal piece, and it's just tied in together on a diagonal screw so that when it was rocking, if it was a little bit off (which such things can be), you still never had any wood touching the floor plane and creating a bump in it.[39]

Tuttle's Nonna Rocking Chair combines the bentwood curves of the Thonet original but adds tubular steel to update the design and to tighten the rocker's movement. Its comfort, traditional lines, and contemporary "feel" have made it one of Strässle's best-selling models, especially to a German market.

The Arco Chair is among Tuttle's most beautiful designs. In 1980 it won both the Pacifica Award (Los Angeles) and the ASID International Product Design Award. The judges' description of the chair captures its essence: "Clean, sweeping lines, good integration of materials and interesting contrast of soft and hard surfaces. There is no sacrifice of function in order to achieve this appealing sculptured chair."[40]

The Arco Chair can be considered the summary statement of Tuttle's experimentation with steel, moving from a complexity of form to an utter simplicity. The graceful arcs of strap steel and their intersection with two arrow-like lengths of tubular steel create an elegant sculptural statement that has been engineered to withstand the rigors of commercial use. The low-slung leather seat is suspended and appears to float in mid-air; the interplay of materials serves as the chair's only ornament.[41] It has been astutely assessed as a "sinuous sculptural form" that respects the properties of steel while responding to the needs of the human body.[42]

The elegance and innovation witnessed in the Arco, Chariot, and Nonna are a tribute to Tuttle's ability to adapt technology to sophisticated and original contemporary designs without sacrificing their distinctive spirit. They work equally well in modern and traditional architectural settings—from a 1930s "period" home with French medieval flourishes to a contemporary Southern California office interior (figs. 1.55, 1.56).

1.55 Family room in private residence,
Santa Barbara, California, 2001
Arco Chairs by Paul Tuttle, 1976,
produced by Strässle International
Coffee table and buffet by Paul Tuttle
produced by Bud Tullis, Solvang,
California, 1999

1.56 Conference room for Investment
Group of Santa Barbara, California
Arco chairs (1976) by Paul Tuttle
produced by Strässle International
Coffee table and bookshelves
by Paul Tuttle produced by Bud Tullis,
Solvang, California, 1992

1.57 Coffee Table (prototype), 1973
Painted tubular steel, glass
Produced by Strässle International,
Switzerland
Collection of Georgia and Ted Funsten

1.58 Lounge Chair and Ottoman, 1974
Powder-coated tubular steel,
ticking upholstery, foam
Produced by Landes Manufacturing,
Los Angeles

1.59 Jazz II Ph.D., 1987
Painted tubular steel, steel mesh, foam
Produced by Strässle International,
Switzerland, with additions by Paul Tuttle
Collection of Julia Emerson

The expressive possibilities of tubular steel allowed Tuttle to create pieces as elegant and sophisticated as his Arco Chair or as playful as several other pieces that were produced either solely in prototype or in very limited production. His prototype Coffee Table of 1973 (fig. 1.57) represents the first use of color to animate the tubular steel of the table's base. The rainbow of colors and the rhythm of the curved supports (each with mirror-image upper and lower bends) add an element of play to the piece. The curves, colors, lines, and textures that were possible with steel were well suited to Tuttle's witty design sensibility.

Around the same time, Tuttle also designed a special line of furniture for Landes Manufacturing of Los Angeles, which included a group of seating and tables made from painted bent tubular steel and cotton "ticking" upholstery (fig. 1.58). This inexpensive line shared the playfulness of the prototype Coffee Table and diverged from the sophistication characteristic of the more expensive furniture produced by Strässle. With this short-lived Landes partnership, Tuttle fulfilled a long-admired Bauhaus ambition of creating quality furniture for a mass market.[43]

Two other whimsical pieces blur the boundary between sculpture and furniture. Tuttle called them his "follies." Tractor Seat Jazz (1977; see fig. 2.26) incorporates a tractor seat and a complex composition of bent tubular steel—both painted by Tuttle in his favorite colors—to function as a playful side chair. Though distinctively his own, Tractor Seat Jazz bears an unmistakable resemblance to the Castiglioni brothers famous but less eccentric Mezzadro Stool, which went into production in 1970 (see fig. 2.27).

As a follow-up to Tractor Seat Jazz, Tuttle created Jazz II Ph.D. (fig. 1.59). This chair is as improvisational in its form as it is in its name. Tuttle quotes from various of his other tubular steel chairs to create the linear composition that becomes the chair's arms and legs. The wire mesh seat is adorned with a painted bull's-eye, and colored foam balls complete the chair's quirky appeal. Jazz II Ph.D. captures the essence of Tuttle's dictum that a sense of fun in a piece of furniture is truly a part of its function.

Tuttle's follies were related to a series of sculptural constructions created in Switzerland in the 1970s during a highly experimental phase of his career. Indeed, several of these sculptures were made for the Strässle family, including a monumental outdoor piece for their garden called Caged Verticals (c. 1970; fig 1.60). Tuttle designed this rebar and steel-pipe sculpture to function like a lightning rod. The simple structure, resembling pick-up sticks inside a circular cage, also became a natural play structure for the six Strässle children. Tuttle's second project for the Strässle residence was a large outdoor sculptural construction (approximately twenty-one feet end-to-end) fabricated out of tubular and strap steel (fig. 1.61a). The sculpture was intended to "rock" gently on a mirrored circle, which would capture the shifting reflection of the piece in reverse (fig. 1.61b).

During the years he worked on contract for Strässle, Tuttle became part of the intellectual community in Switzerland, spending time with writers Thomas Mann and Alfred Andersch and artists Mark Tobey, Ben Nicholson, Jean Arp, and Italo Valenti—among others. Tuttle gravitated to artistic and literary figures and brought to the table his own keen observations and artistic sensitivities. Just as Santa Barbara provided him a liberated creative haven, so too did the places he chose to live within Switzerland. He resided only briefly in Kirchberg, the small provincial village that was home to Strässle International and the Strässle family. For five years he spent most of his time in the Ticino, the southern, Italian-speaking region of Switzerland, where he lived in the tiny hill town of Incella, overlooking Lake Maggiore. This provided a home base

1.60 Caged Verticals, c. 1970
Rebar and steel
Strässle residence, Kirchberg,
Switzerland

1.61a, b Paul Tuttle working on a sculptural construction at the Strässle residence, Kirchberg, Switzerland, 1970s. Another view of the same piece appears below.

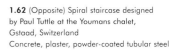

1.62 (Opposite) Spiral staircase designed by Paul Tuttle at the Youmans chalet, Gstaad, Switzerland
Concrete, plaster, powder-coated tubular steel

1.63a–c A number of Tuttle's furniture designs appear throughout the Youmans chalet in Rougemont, Switzerland: (Top) A custom dining table with Zeta Dining Chairs; (bottom, left) Fat Tube Table; (bottom, right) a Circle Chair combined with a nineteenth-century Austrian writing desk adorned with a Chinese lacquer-ware box and tea caddy.

as beautiful as the one he had in Santa Barbara. About every two weeks he would take the train to Kirchberg to work at the factory for several days and then return to the Ticino.

Tuttle also spent eight months in Gstaad, Switzerland, working on a project for designers Valerie and Scott Youmans, whom he had met in California in 1961.[44] The Youmans moved to Gstaad in 1962 and transformed a classic chalet, which they called La Haute Grange, into a remarkable year-round home. Although traditional on the exterior, they completely remodeled the interior, opening up the spaces and raising ceiling heights to create "the antithesis of the typical Swiss chalet in which small rooms, small windows and low ceilings are the norm."[45] They invited Tuttle to design a circular staircase that would link the three levels of the chalet (fig. 1.62). Beginning in the lower level, it progressed up through the main floor to the loft gallery above. Made of poured concrete and covered in white plaster, the treads of the staircase appear to float in space. The beautiful sweeps of the bent tubular steel railing emphasize the spiral form and lead the eye up through the open interior of the chalet. This staircase-cum-sculpture fits within Tuttle's period of intense exploration of tubular steel—testing its structural capabilities, its ability to create a powerful linear composition, and its harmonious combination with other materials.

In 1980 the Youmans purchased another piece of property with an original seventeenth-century chalet a few miles from Gstaad in the village of Rougemont.[46] As a part of its total restoration, Tuttle designed a similar spiral staircase but without the vertical sweep of the original. The Youmans included in the interior design several pieces of furniture that Tuttle had designed for Strässle, including the Zeta Chairs, a Circle Chair, and an Anaconda Table (figs. 1.63a–c). They are creatively combined with antiques and the

Youmans's eclectic art collection. Additionally, Tuttle created a sculptural construction for them called *The Weed* (1971; see half-title page) based on the bent tubular steel structure of his Circle Chair of 1970. Painted green, the artist referred to it as "a piece of joy" because its lines exude happiness, and "a piece of nonsense" because it has no function other than to please.

Although his contractual agreement with Strässle International ended in 1983 when Tuttle reached the Swiss retirement age of 65, he continued to work on a royalty basis and designed several new pieces in the 1980s and 1990s. Because the 1980s marked Tuttle's shift in emphasis to custom design work for clients in Santa Barbara, there was a complementary dynamic between what he was doing in California and the new designs he proposed for Strässle. For example, a highly inventive design that was never put into production but was intended as an accompaniment to the Arco Chair is the Munira Coffee Table. Two versions exist: one in marble as a prototype for Strässle and a second of polished aluminum created as a commission in Santa Barbara (1981; figs. 1.64a, b). The custom version has the kind of flexibility Tuttle sought for many of his designs: the three polished aluminum segments of the table base can be kept together or moved apart and used with or without a glass top.

In 1994 Strässle introduced Tuttle's Nenufar Easy Chair (fig. 1.66), which was based on a an exploratory piece he produced in Santa Barbara in 1993 called the "V" Armchair (figs. 1.65a, b). The prototype armchair's unique openwork structure was made of painted tubular steel, and the deep "V" of the frame was filled with two upholstered-foam seat cushions and one back cushion. The Nenufar substitutes bold primary colors for the subtle blue and purple of the prototype. It also corrects what Tuttle saw as a visual interruption in the stacking of two cushions

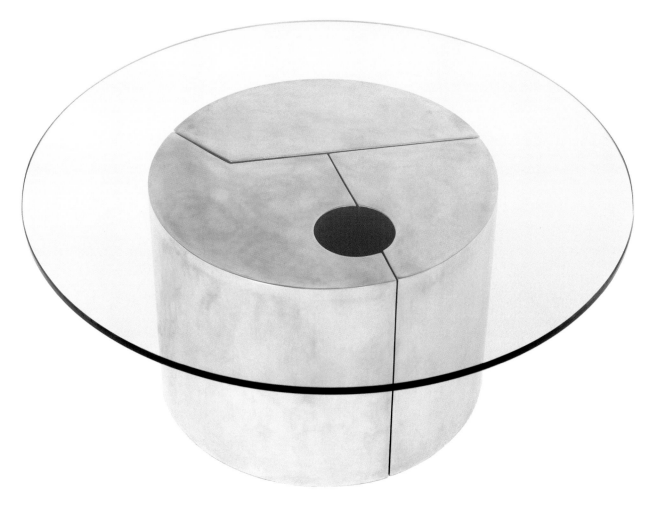

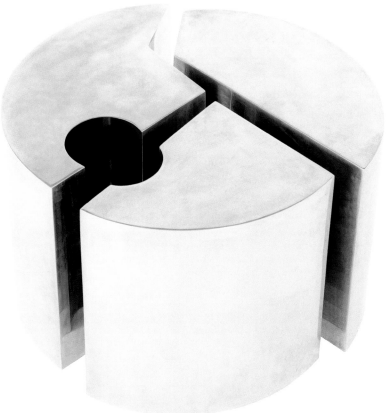

1.64a, b Munira Coffee Table, 1981
Polished aluminum, paint, glass
Produced by Specialty Welding,
Santa Barbara, California
Collection of Alma and Paul Gray

1.65a, b (Left, top and bottom)
"V" Armchair, 1993
Powder-coated tubular steel, foam, ultrasuede
Produced by Spike Pollorena, Paradise
Mobile Welding, Santa Barbara, California
Collection of Carol Valentine

1.66 (Above)
Nenufar Easy Chair, 1994
Powder-coated tubular steel, foam, leather
Produced by Strässle International,
Switzerland.

1.67a, b Super "V" Armchair, 1994
Appleply, stainless steel, ultrasuede upholstery
Produced by Bud Tullis, Solvang, California
Collection of Yelda and Paul Recsei

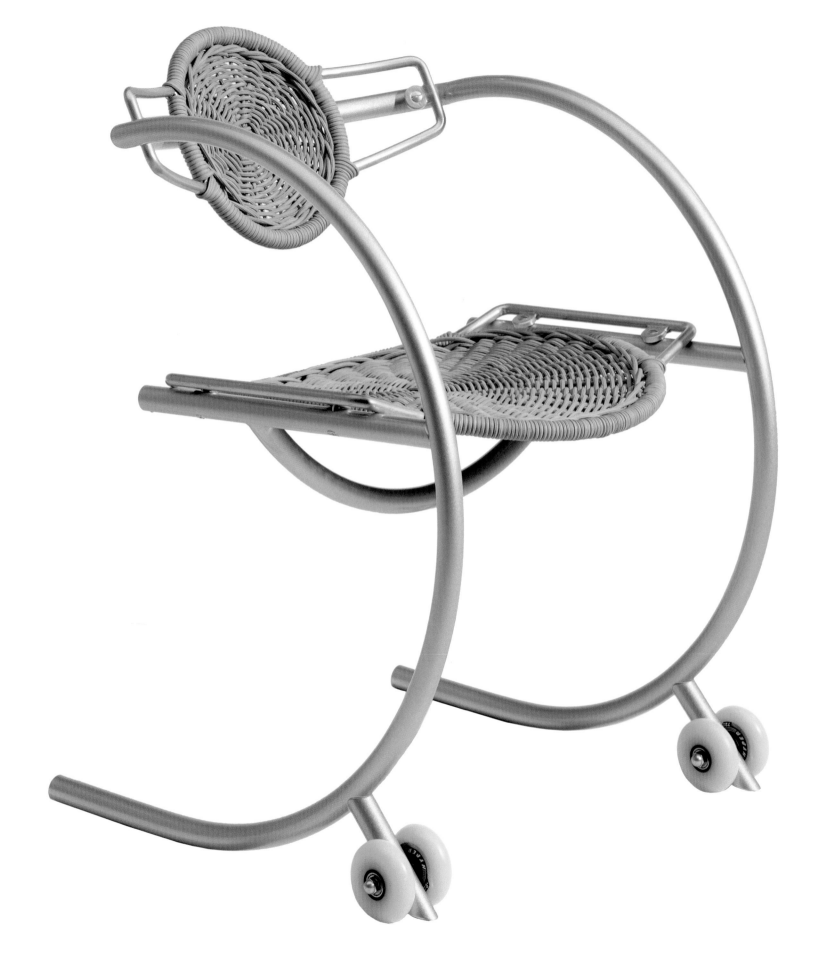

for the seat by having one deep V-shaped form. As assembled by Strässle, the color contrast between the steel frame and the leather upholstery gives these chairs Tuttle's signature playfulness. To illustrate how ideas central to a production model could reverberate in a unique piece for the custom market, Tuttle designed the Super "V" Armchair in 1994 (figs. 1.67a, b). It replaced the steel of the Nenufar with a beautiful laminated appleply frame, which emphasizes the geometric shape with a broad sweep of wood and provides a perfect complement to the chair's dramatic red ultrasuede upholstery. The chair's strong sculptural form is equally striking from the back, where small details interrupt its plain geometry.

In 1993 Tuttle designed a popular line of indoor/outdoor furniture for Strässle called the Skate Series, which developed out of a side chair that was originally produced in Santa Barbara as a custom piece. The Skate Series was initially produced in the United States under license to Atelier International. Chairs, tables, and a chaise longue comprise the series. The chair is Tuttle's homage to "the integrity of the circle," especially evident in the lines of the zinc-plated and powder-coated tubular steel frame and the form of the seat back (fig. 1.68). It has been said that the chair has an emphatic "California" look derived from the colorful use of rollerblade wheels and the playfulness of its overall form. The use of wheels to "roll a woman up to the table" was an additional amusement for Tuttle:

I come out of that generation where a gentleman helped a lady up to the table. And so I couldn't think of a good reason not to roll her up! And so, seriously, that's how the rollerblade wheels came into it. And also they were such simple forms, and they were in colors. Now they're getting chic and everything goes black or transparent or whatever…. That's how it evolved. And then the whole series of accessory items completed the idea of it. And the thing wasn't out six months before we got awards on it. And then Atelier International didn't make any more.[47]

A final design Tuttle created for Strässle in 1997 culminates his experimentation with the dramatic contrast between chrome-plated steel and black leather. Called the Padaro Chair (fig. 1.69) after the street where Tuttle lived in Carpinteria while the chair was being designed, it is reminiscent of Mies van der Rohe's famous Barcelona Chair (see fig. 2.2). Tuttle engineered the strap steel to wrap around a wide tube of steel to provide support for the seat and back. This has also allowed him to achieve a longer cantilever and to extend the front legs in a graceful curve that complicates what was a symmetrical design in the Barcelona Chair. There is a modernist reduction in the lines of Tuttle's Padaro as well as in the treatment of the smooth leather upholstery. Unfortunately, this chair has had little exposure outside of Europe, although it would seem to have the potential for substantial success elsewhere, especially in the contract market in the United States.

THE SANTA BARBARA YEARS

Although Tuttle had lived in Santa Barbara since 1956 and was a member of the city's small but active artists' community, his freelance career there did not gain momentum until after a "retrospective" exhibition was held by the Santa Barbara Museum of Art in 1978 (fig. 1.85).[48] A number of Tuttle's important designs from the 1950s and 1960s were shown, but the clear objective of this exhibition was to introduce the community to the heretofore unseen pieces he had produced for Strässle International in the 1970s. Most of the pieces Strässle shipped out for the show were purchased by local collectors or were kept by Tuttle in his own residence (fig. 1.86), which became something of a small gallery. A feature story appeared in the *Los Angeles Times* in conjunction with the exhibition, bringing Tuttle recognition for his furniture and his architecture.[49]

1.68 Skate Dining Chair, 1993
Painted steel, synthetic rattan, rollerblade wheels
Produced by Strässle International, Switzerland
Distributed by Janus et Cie., Los Angeles, California
Collection of the University Art Museum,
UCSB, Gift of Maria and Alex Strässle

1.69 (Opposite) **Padaro Chair**, 1997
Chrome-plated tubular and strap steel, leather
Produced by Strässle International, Switzerland
Collection of the University Art Museum, UCSB,
Gift of Maria and Alex Strässle

1.70 Installation view of the exhibiton
Paul Tuttle Designer, held at the
Santa Barbara Museum of Art, 1978

1.71 Paul Tuttle and Bud Tullis's logo inlaid on the underside of a custom furniture design.

1.72 Paul Tuttle at home, Santa Barbara, California, 1978

1.73 China "X" Table, 1983
Cherry, painted tubular steel, glass, Italian bicycle sprocket
Produced by Bud Tullis, Solvang, California, and Specialty Welding, Santa Barbara, California
Collection of Jon and Lillian Lovelace

The year 1981 marked an important transition in Tuttle's freelance career. In that year he met master craftsman Bud Tullis through Carolyn Watson, who owned a gallery in Santa Barbara where Tuttle's work was exhibited. Tullis, a resident of nearby Solvang, California, had long admired Tuttle's designs and had seen exhibitions of his early work in Pasadena. Tullis began producing Paul's custom furniture in 1982, and their highly productive and sympathetic working relationship over the next twenty years yielded over two hundred unique furniture designs. Each Tuttle-Tullis piece was "signed" with an engraved "T-T" (fig. 1.71). In addition to the client-driven pieces they produced, Tuttle also designed new work on a purely exploratory basis, which was exhibited annually beginning in 1982 in local galleries or in private showings in his own design studio, the Design Source (see fig. 2.1). Generally featuring from six to ten new pieces these shows and the publicity they attracted became a vehicle for sales as well as for building Tuttle's private clientele.

Even though Tuttle continued to spend at least three months a year in Switzerland until the mid-1990s, Santa Barbara provided the perfect environment to foster his creativity. "The sense of the environment here—the wonderful light, the ocean, the almost Mediterranean landscape—gives me the freedom to design furniture that is as authentic as I can make it."[50] Designing for a private market was also liberating for Tuttle. He could avoid the compromises necessary to meet the requirements of industrial production. Instead he was able to explore fully the kinds of design challenges that had long fascinated him: "With every new piece I'm looking for another experience.... I'm still starved to death to learn. I mean I am so curious. In some strange way,... I still don't think I was ever meant to be doing what I'm doing. How can you explain that?"[51] There is a clear dialogue between the custom work commissioned by clients and the pieces Tuttle produced in what he called a purely exploratory mode:

I have the need to feel the environment and to have some real insight into how they [clients] intend to use the furniture. I need to have the time with the people themselves in their environment. And then I pretty much take it from there. I, of course, inquire about the materials, and I usually know that beforehand because if people come to me, I usually know something about them.... Their needs are for the most part unlike anyone else's—there may be generalizations, but there are still differences. The design then pretty much takes care of itself....

And in doing the custom things, of course, you discover certain things about yourself. This has to do with the way I solve their problem, if they've got a problem. I sometimes surprise them with the solutions I come up with, and so that opens up a Pandora's box of my own curiosities of wanting to find, to have an experience, that will put to use something from a previous design.[52]

In response to the freedom he encountered in working for a custom clientele, Tuttle spent twenty years pursuing several specific design problems, some solved in a series of iterations that can be called "evolutions."[53] Additionally, he produced a number of one-of-a-kind pieces that were self-contained design exercises undertaken to satisfy his own curiosity or in response to previously produced, client-driven requests. Tuttle's Santa Barbara years were enormously fertile and investigatory, particularly as he found a way to explore fully the tension between structural concepts and material possibilities in seating, tables, and other interior furnishings. This goal differed little from what he had determined to do at the outset of his career, except that now he had greater latitude to push his designs into new territories and to pursue particular problems until he himself was satisfied with their solution. Tuttle was his own harshest critic, never letting consumer admiration lead him into complacency or deter him from meeting his own high standards. His insecurities as a designer kept

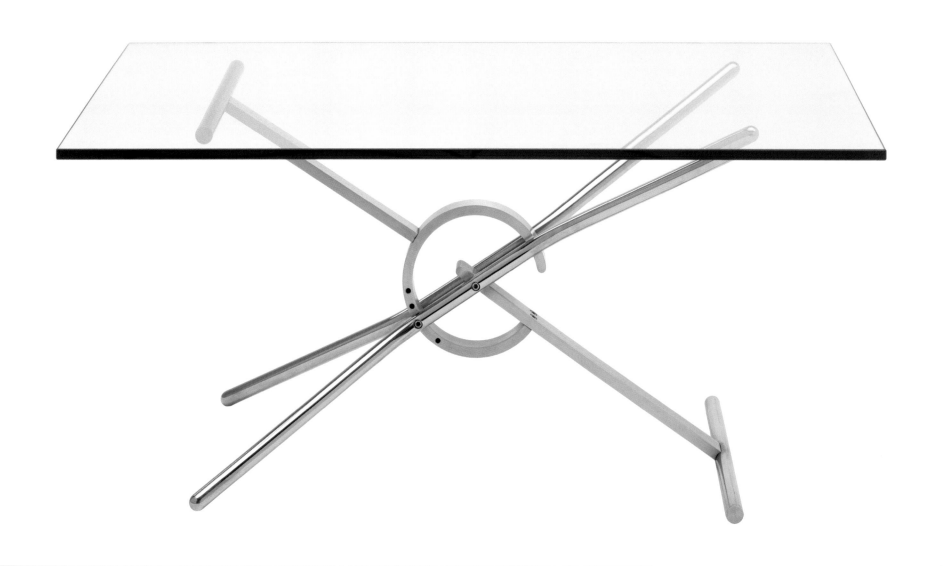

1.74 Flexible "X" Table, 1983
Aluminum, stainless steel, glass
Produced by Specialty Welding,
Santa Barbara, California
Collection of Candice and Farshid Assassi

1.75 "X" Chair, 1982
Cherry, leather, tubular steel
Produced by Bud Tullis,
Solvang, California

him perpetually on a quest for achievements of his own invention: "I don't believe I have a definite opinion of what good design is but it should incorporate the fulfillment of an original intent along with a distinct spirit and vitality."[54]

Basic to much of his custom work is the combination of wood and metal, which Tuttle viewed as an ideal structural collaboration. The metal adds strength and luster while the wood contributes texture and warmth. "Basically at heart I am a wood person because of the richness of it, and I am oriented to it in the sense of the organic. But my absolute intrigue and fascination with what I could do with metal when I discovered it [led me to use] metal oftentimes as much, if not more, than I did wood—simply because of the structure it gave me."[55]

The legitimacy of his personal design exploration was reinforced by an Independent Artist Award in Design that he received from the National Endowment for the Arts in 1982. Using the award funds, Tuttle produced several exploratory works, beginning with the China "X" Table (1982–1983; fig. 1.73). This table's base incorporates a bicycle sprocket used to adjust its height so it can function as a coffee table, cocktail table, or small dining/serving table. The slender steel rods that help support the table's glass top are painted bright colors and look, as one reviewer remarked, like a child's pick-up sticks.[56] Tuttle described the table as "a happy thing, a piece with fun, color and abstraction."[57]

At the same time he produced two related pieces, the "X" Chair (1982; fig. 1.75) and the Flexible "X" Table (1983; fig. 1.74). The "X" Chair combines ideas from some of his earlier pieces, such as the Anaconda Chair (see fig. 1.47), but reveals how he incorporated the X formation in steel.

The Flexible "X" Table has a base constructed of tubular steel with an aluminum center to accommodate adjustments. While using a structural principle similar to that employed in the China "X" Table, the cool metal and glass—instead of the warmth of wood—create a very different result, replacing whimsy with elegance.

Of the pieces Tuttle created with NEA grant funds, the most complicated is a Chaise Longue of 1982 in which he solved the problem of adjusting the angle of the back by using a quick release axle from a ten-speed Italian racing bicycle (fig. 1.76). As in the China "X" Table, Tuttle revealed his ingenuity by adapting a mechanism from another category of engineering to a piece of furniture. Moreover, as the designer himself put it, "A bicycle part is a beautiful thing," referring as much to its ornamental aspect as to its practicality and relative affordability.[58] A photograph taken at Specialty Welding, the Santa Barbara company that fabricated the steel, reveals the chaise's elegant lines and the simplicity of Tuttle's structural solution (fig. 1.78). The richness of the wood base element and the softness of the dark purple ultrasuede complete its distinctive design.

Tuttle produced five more chaise longues over the years, mostly as exploratory pieces, working to simplify the structure, enhance the sleekness of the design, and test various upholstery materials from fabric to cane to leather (figs. 1.93, 1.94; see also fig. 1.145). Whereas his final designs are made in leather and cane, his most distinctive example is the Dragster Lounge (1988; fig. 1.94). It was inspired by a dragster race car and Tuttle's fantasy of being a race-car driver. As he recounted, "I think Formula 1 racing is the finest union of man and machine."[59] The form and details of this lounge further demonstrate Tuttle's desire to inject humor and spirit into his work.

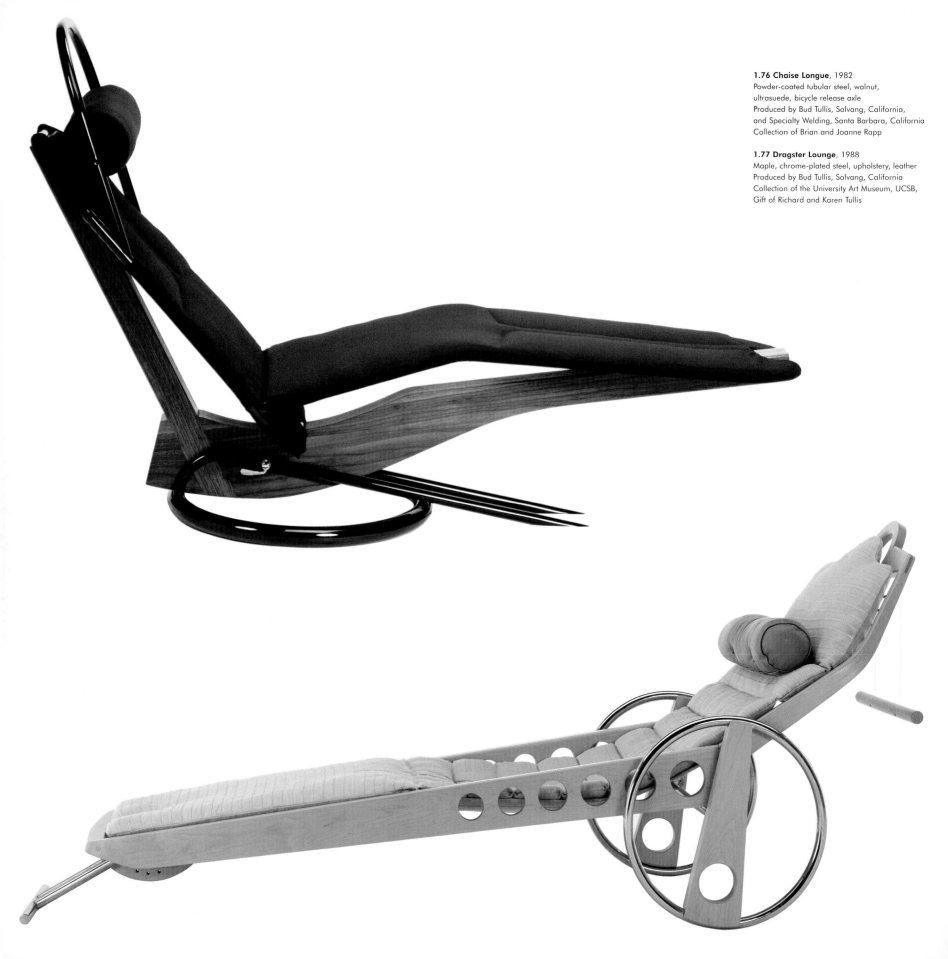

1.76 Chaise Longue, 1982
Powder-coated tubular steel, walnut,
ultrasuede, bicycle release axle
Produced by Bud Tullis, Solvang, California,
and Specialty Welding, Santa Barbara, California
Collection of Brian and Joanne Rapp

1.77 Dragster Lounge, 1988
Maple, chrome-plated steel, upholstery, leather
Produced by Bud Tullis, Solvang, California
Collection of the University Art Museum, UCSB,
Gift of Richard and Karen Tullis

1.78 Paul Tuttle at Specialty Welding,
Santa Barbara, California, with the tubular steel
frame for his Chaise Longue of 1982 (1.76)

1.79 Chaise Longue, 1996
Maple, cane, tubular steel, cushion
Produced by Bud Tullis, Solvang, California;
steel fabrication by Spike Pollorena, Paradise
Mobile Welding, Santa Barbara, California
Collection of the Andina Family

1.80 "T85" Rocking Chair, 1985
Beech, tubular steel, leather
Produced by Bud Tullis, Solvang, California
Collection of Mandy and Cliff Einstein

1.81 Rocking Chair, 1997
Cherry, painted steel, leather
Produced by Bud Tullis, Solvang,California;
steel fabrication by Spike Pollorena, Paradise
Mobile Welding, Santa Barbara, California
Collection of Danielle and John Crowder

As with the reclining lounge, which he began designing in 1972 for Strässle, he was also interested in developing new ideas for the rocking chair. In addition to the Nonna, which has been a best-seller for Strässle for nearly thirty years, he designed two other rockers. One, his "T85" Rocking Chair, was designed as a prototype for possible industrial production by Strässle (fig. 1.80). In it Tuttle used the same combination of tubular steel, wood, and leather that had appeared in the Nonna, but he removed the visual reference to the Thonet classic by replacing the loop of the armrest-rocker element with a more orthogonal form. Nevertheless, the circle is retained in the clever cut-out that helps to form the "T85" armrest. A final rocker was produced on "spec" in 1997 and represents one of Tuttle's most complex sculptural statements (fig. 1.81). It combines rich cherry wood, natural leather, and black powder-coated steel in an elegant interplay of solids and voids, darks and lights, which despite the rocker's nod to an ergonomically formed seat and back, seems too gorgeous for actual use.

Tables—especially coffee tables and side tables with their smaller proportions—preoccupied Tuttle because of the possibilities they offered for pure sculptural expression. He concentrated on the composition of the base as well as on the form of the top, often preferring glass for its transparency. As early as 1984, and continuing throughout his career, Tuttle designed glass tabletops in beautiful free-form shapes, which he drew at full size, laboring over the flow of the lines.[60] Their irregularity is a mark of Tuttle's insistence on the handcrafted, even if the tubular steel of many bases was machined (fig. 1.82). The combination of glass and steel was one of his favorites, emphasizing a purity of line and material. Many of his tables, however, add the warmth and texture of wood, which remained Tuttle's preferred material even if only for dramatic accent. One particularly elegant Coffee Table of 1993 (fig. 1.83) combines a free-form glass top with a strap-steel base

and adds a single dramatic cylinder of purpleheart to serve as a leg support. The graceful lines of the glass top are accentuated by the asymmetrical, linear pattern of the strap-steel understructure, especially when viewed from the top. The appeal of Tuttle's coffee tables as sculpture lies in their formal beauty as observed from several vantage points (fig. 1.84). By contrast, when the table top was wood, Tuttle frequently used other design strategies to reveal the underlying structure. From his first coffee table of 1950 (see fig. 1.4), which used wood plugs to mark the configuration of the leg supports on an otherwise uninterrupted mahogany top, Tuttle has used an interpenetration of forms to expose structure. In many examples a slash of contrasting wood reveals the line of the base beneath and creates a distinctive compositional accent (figs. 1.85, 1.86). In more recent years he incorporated prefabricated cylinders of plywood into his bases. These could be variously veneered and arranged in unusual compositions that read differently from the top and the side (fig. 1.87). Other of his occasional tables are pure fun, with leg supports forming a spiral or a circle (figs. 1.88, 1.89), echoing the spirit of his early experimental wrought-iron Spiral Table (see fig. 1.17).

Dining tables, because of their size, were produced largely as commissions for clients. As noted previously Tuttle always considered his clients' lifestyles and personalities even while fulfilling his own design intentions. Many tables reveal his interest in flexibility, finding ways to satisfy more than one purpose. One dining table has drop leaves on two sides so that its top can be triangular or circular. Others have hinged gatelegs that allow the table to expand or contract in size (fig. 1.90). Many, like the tables described earlier that were made for Doetsch, Grether in Basel, have glass insets in the wood tops so that the base below can be seen and so that the fluid plane of the top surface is visually interrupted. Other dining tables have graceful free-form tops, like Tuttle's coffee tables, which give them his handcrafted signature look (fig. 1.91).

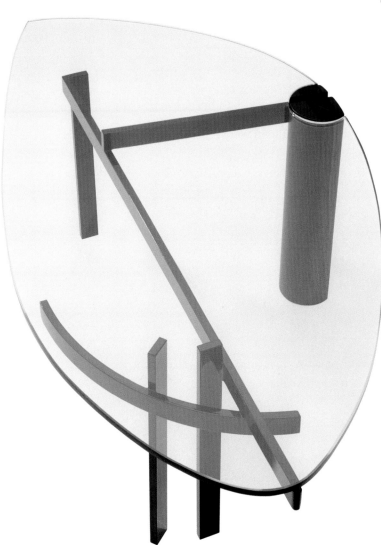

1.82 Coffee Table, 2001
Zebrawood, painted steel, glass
Produced by Bud Tullis, Solvang, California
Collection of the University Art Museum,
UCSB, Architecture and Design Collection,
Gift of the artist

1.83 Coffee Table, 1993
Purpleheart, steel, glass
Produced by Bud Tullis, Solvang, California,
and Spike Pollorena, Paradise Mobile Welding,
Santa Barbara, California
Collection of Priscilla K. Giesen

1.84 Coffee Table, 1994
Purpleheart, powder-coated steel, glass
Produced by Bud Tullis, Solvang, California,
and Spike Pollorena, Paradise
Mobile Welding, Santa Barbara, California
Collection of Maureen Murphy

1.85 (Top) **Coffee Table**, 1989
Honduran mahogany, rosewood, glass
Produced by Bud Tullis, Solvang, California
Collection of Gary Wooten

1.86 (Bottom) **Coffee Table**, 1988
Cherry, walnut, chrome-plated steel, glass
Produced by Bud Tullis, Solvang, California
Collection of Jill Vander Hoof

1.87 (Opposite) **Coffee Table**, 2000
Purpleheart, walnut, painted steel
Produced by Bud Tullis, Solvang, California
Collection of the Duca Family

1.88 (Top) **Shell Table**, 1987
Cherry, metal
Produced by Bud Tullis, Solvang, California
Collection of Robert and Ann Diener

1.89 (Bottom) **Table with Fifteen Legs**, 1993
Cherry, painted tubular steel, painted wood, glass
Produced by Bud Tullis, Solvang, California
Collection of Joan and Bill Crawford

1.90 Dining Table, 1990
Cherry, glass, metal
Produced by Bud Tullis, Solvang, California
Collection of Jill Vander Hoof

1.91 (Top) **Dining Table**, 1988
Cherry, tinted glass
Produced by Bud Tullis, Solvang, California
Collection of Paul and Evan Turpin

1.92 (Bottom) **Dining Table**, 1989
Marble, chrome-plated steel, glass
Steel fabrication by Jeff Walker and marble
by Donald Davis, Santa Barbara, California
Collection of Candice and Farshid Assassi

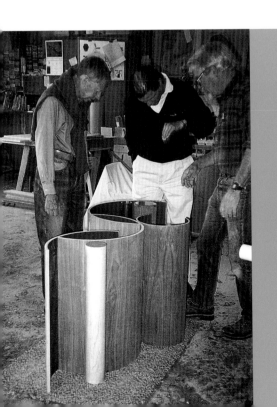

1.93 Dining Table, 1996
Plywood, walnut, formica,
powder-coated steel, glass
Produced by Bud Tullis, Solvang, California
Collection of the Andina Family

1.94 Paul Tuttle and Bud Tullis
at the Tullis workshop, Solvang, California,
in 1996, discussing with Francesco Andina
(center) the fabrication of the dining table
commissioned for the Andina family (fig. 1.93).

Whether in glass or in wood, Tuttle always drew the shape of the top at full-scale to ensure that the form was absolutely "right" and harmonious with the base.

Because Tuttle's tables are often as much sculpture as they are functional objects, he exploited their material possibilities in innovative ways. One table combines marble, glass, and a bold sweep of chrome-plated tubular steel (fig. 1.92). Intended originally for dining, it has been effectively adapted for use as a computer table (see figs. 1.115a, b). As with the most recent coffee tables, several dining tables incorporated large wood cylinders either in the round or as hemispheres to create a base that works in three and two dimensions depending on viewpoint (figs. 1.93, 1.94).

Although the variety of the tables Tuttle designed is remarkable, the real emphasis of his design exploration was seating, most notably chairs. Tuttle's need to design an authentic three-legged chair and to find the right balance in its form, structure, and materials occupied him intermittently over a twenty-five year period, beginning in 1970.[61] In his Three-Legged Chair of 1984 (fig. 1.95) the two front legs, arm, and backrest are one continuous laminated piece of walnut, much like his "X" Chair of 1982 (see fig. 1.75). The tubular steel back leg is an elongated inverted "Y," replacing the "X" of the earlier version. In 1995 Tuttle returned to the problem (fig. 1.96), reprising the essential lines of his Strässle-produced Anaconda but creating a distinctive molded-wood seat and back. Here the contrast of the steel with the rich mahogany is tempered by the former's solar black powder-coating. Additionally, the structural system Tuttle devised for joining the seat to the three legs becomes a fluid part of the chair's total design.

Although not strictly a part of the three-legged chair evolution, Tuttle's Spring Chair (1991; see fig 2.35) was, in his estimation, his only "true" three-legged chair as it has only three contact points with the floor. The turned and laminated arc of birch plywood gives the chair heft and strength, while the strap steel of the third leg gives the chair its "spring." The choice of a bold aquamarine ultrasuede is not only a beautiful counterpoint to the light wood but is typical of Tuttle's exuberant sensibility. The way he used materials in this chair was a notable advance in his design exploration:

For me the new experience was to continue to try to educate myself, discover a keener edge to what I could do with materials and how far I could take them, maybe a bit further than what I had learned from the previous thing which was done. I mean, the Spring Chair is a perfect illustration of that: how far I could take and bend wood and get a natural spring in it. A form that somehow would really work for me. I mean, for instance, Alvar Aalto who used wood in this way, his things were always of dimension, and also they were always made of beech wood, which bends naturally. My things were taken to a much smaller dimension in that area, and also all the things I have done like that have metal, again in combination, not strictly a wood thing. I mean, we have never, neither Bud [Tullis] nor I, ever had the real opportunity to explore areas other than what you could explore with very limited equipment.[62]

A second design preoccupation for Tuttle was his "66" Series Chair. There is certainly a dialogue between the evolution of the "66" Series Chair and the Three-Legged Chair—both share the same combination of materials but explore two different structural systems. Developing

1.95 Three-Legged Chair, 1984
Walnut, cane, chrome-plated tubular steel
Produced by Bud Tullis, Solvang, California,
and Specialty Welding, Santa Barbara, California
Collection of Candice and Farshid Assassi

1.96 Three-Legged Chair, 1995
Mahogany, painted tubular steel
Produced by Bud Tullis, Solvang, California,
and Spike Pollorena, Paradise Mobile
Welding, Santa Barbara, California
Collection of Candice and Farshid Assassi

1.97 "66/85" Dining Chair, 1985
Maple, cherry, cane, painted steel
Produced by Bud Tullis, Solvang, California
Collection of Paul and Alma Gray

1.98 "66/95" Chair, 1997
Maple, stainless steel
Produced by Bud Tullis, Solvang, California
Collection of the University Art Museum,
UCSB, Gift of the artist

out of the first chair he designed in 1966 for the Youmans in Switzerland (see fig. 1.21), **Tuttle's "66/85" Chair** (fig. 1.97) has the same inverted Y-shaped legs and depends on the insertion of a U-shaped steel "brace" to attach and support the seat, here made in wood and cane. Tuttle and Bud Tullis struggled over the proportional relationship between the wood and the gauge of the steel, balancing structural demands with aesthetic priorities. According to Tullis:

Paul wanted the metal thin so we made one, and the welder and I both thought it was too weak because if you start rocking in the chair, the metal would bend. And I think I told Paul, and he said, "No, we're going to do it this way." Well, we built the first one, and it did—it just bent and it stayed there. So we took it back, and we straightened it, and it happened again. And I think by then we had made two or three of them, until we finally talked him into using the next thicker metal. So we recalled all of them, and I redid them for free. OK. And we had to go in, and I had to figure out how to make that space [between the legs] an eighth of an inch bigger to fit the bar. And I figured out a way of doing it. But, see he agonized over that eighth of an inch. It took awhile for him to see it. And that became a very popular chair. I think I made quite a few of them, and it worked fine after we did that. We never had a problem.[63]

Tuttle struggled over the width of the steel brace in the "66/85" chair because the structural elements were so integral to its design. The three bolts that join the wood and steel in the legs also become ornamentation and balance the three cherry inlays that join the two pieces of the back rail. To complete the composition, Tuttle's design called for inlaid strips of cherry in the tips of the legs. The arms, which point sharply forward, nicely balance with their tapered ends the graceful curve in the chair's legs. The uniqueness of this design, along with its simplicity and comfort, has made it very popular as a dining chair. Tullis

produced it in a large edition using maple, cherry, and purpleheart along with the steel elements chrome-plated or powder-coated black (see also fig. 2.28).

Tuttle was not fully satisfied with the 1985 design solution, however, and ten years later introduced the "66/95" version, which shows a reduction in form and a simplification in materials and details (fig. 1.98). The strategic U-shaped steel brace is thicker and strictly orthogonal. While the joinery details of the backrest have been retained, the "bolt" elements attaching the wood to the steel are more exaggerated cylinders—repeated in exposed wood plugs covering the places where the steel supports are bolted to the seat. Perhaps the most radical change in the 1995 version of the chair is the sharp abbreviation of the armrests, making their upper edges contiguous with the legs. The chair has become overall a stronger more coherent sculptural statement, especially in the use of maple and the way its exposed grain patterns contrast with the high-tech edginess of the steel.

The third important design evolution of Tuttle's career is that of the "Z" chair, which developed over a thirty-two year period beginning with his first cantilevered chair of 1964 and ending with the Super "Z" chair of 1996.[64] The number of versions that were produced during this long period reveal how Tuttle never tired of the experimental process nor of the effort to get it "right" (figs. 1.99a–d). After a hiatus of more than twenty years, Tuttle returned to the Z-shaped cantilever in 1989 and reworked the steel frame as well as the seat and back elements. Gone was the upholstered comfort of the original; instead the design incorporated rolled aluminum for the seat and back (fig. 1.99b). Obviously no longer a comfortable chair for lounging, it provided Tuttle with a way to play with the lines and edges of the strap steel and their relationship to the curved planes of the aluminum seat and back piece, which

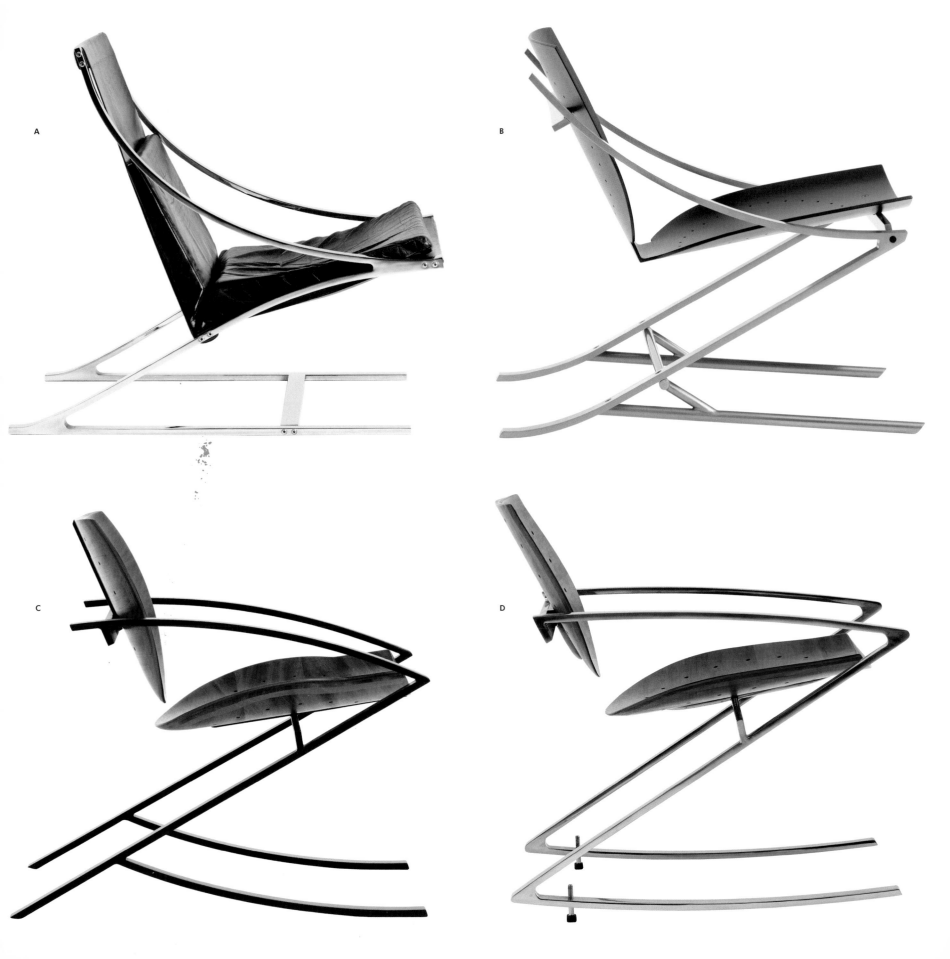

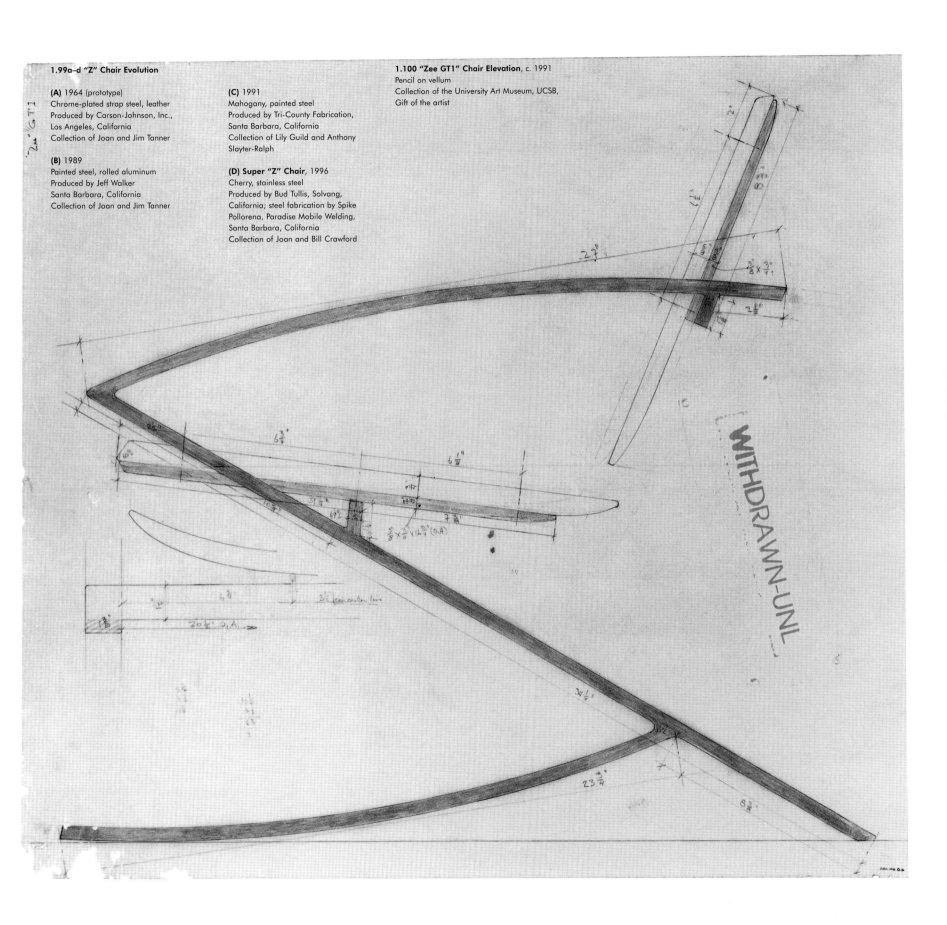

1.99a–d "Z" Chair Evolution

(A) 1964 (prototype)
Chrome-plated strap steel, leather
Produced by Carson-Johnson, Inc.,
Los Angeles, California
Collection of Joan and Jim Tanner

(B) 1989
Painted steel, rolled aluminum
Produced by Jeff Walker
Santa Barbara, California
Collection of Joan and Jim Tanner

(C) 1991
Mahogany, painted steel
Produced by Tri-County Fabrication,
Santa Barbara, California
Collection of Lily Guild and Anthony
Slayter-Ralph

(D) Super "Z" Chair, 1996
Cherry, stainless steel
Produced by Bud Tullis, Solvang,
California; steel fabrication by Spike
Pollorena, Paradise Mobile Welding,
Santa Barbara, California
Collection of Joan and Bill Crawford

1.100 "Zee GT1" Chair Elevation, c. 1991
Pencil on vellum
Collection of the University Art Museum, UCSB,
Gift of the artist

1.101 (Left) **Chair**, 1994
Zebrawood, stainless steel
Produced by Bud Tullis, Solvang, California;
steel fabrication by Tri-County Fabrication,
Santa Barbara, California
Collection of Margaret J. Dent

1.102 (Above) **"Fat Tube" Chair (prototype)**, 1996
Maple cylinder, painted tubular steel,
wool upholstery
Produced by Bud Tullis, Solvang, California
Private Collection

1.103 (Opposite) **Laminated Low Chair**, 2000
Walnut, steel, leather
Produced by Bud Tullis, Solvang, California
Collection of Jill and Barry Kitnick

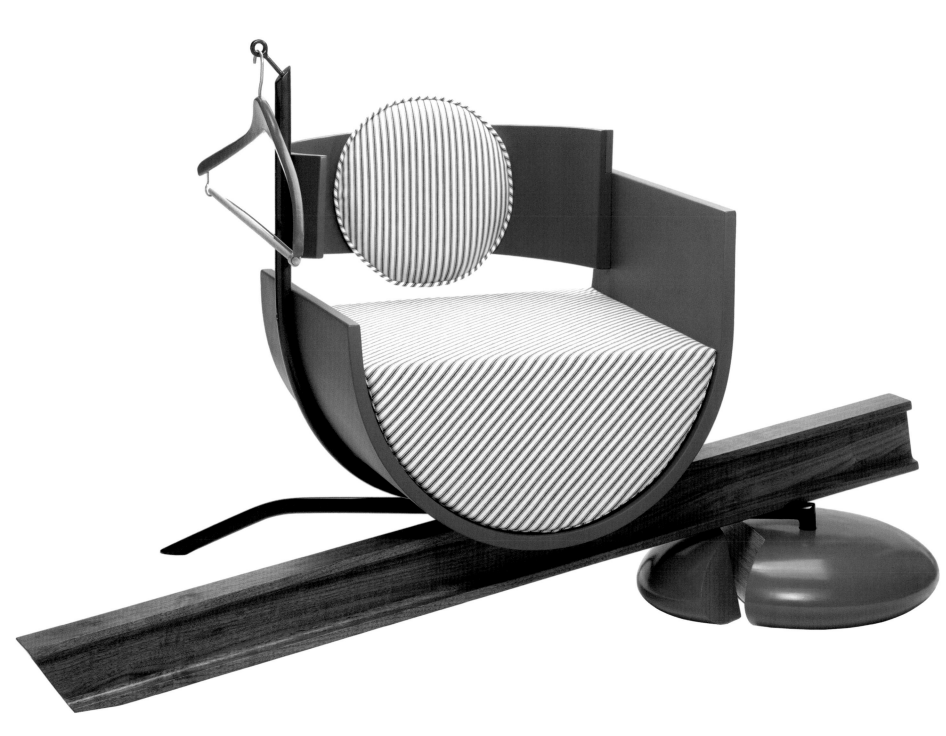

1.104 Tuttle's Folly (English Folly), 1990
Mahogany, painted wood, tubular steel,
upholstery, hanger
Produced by Bud Tullis, Solvang, California
Collection of Candice and Farshid Assassi

1.105 Coop Himmelblau
Vodöl Chair, 1989
Varnished steel, brushed steel, leather
Vitra Design Museum, Weil am Rhein

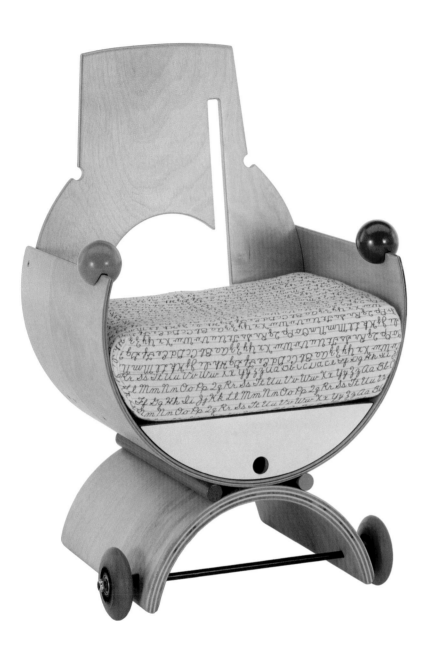

1.106 Baby Folly, 1995
Birch plywood, painted wood,
rollerblade wheels
Produced by Bud Tullis,
Solvang, California
Collection of Erin Reinecke Balint
and John Balint

1.107 The Comic Chair, 2001
Walnut, painted steel,
high-tech wheels
Produced by Bud Tullis,
Solvang, California
Collection of the Duca Family

was contoured to receive the body. In 1991 Tuttle began a series of modifications to the frame and to the shape and alignment of the now separate seat and back elements, which he produced in molded wood (fig. 1.100). This shift lightened the design, bringing to the chair Tuttle's favored combination of cool metal with warm wood and minimizing the structural connections between the two materials. In the " Z" Chair iterations Tuttle played with the gesture of the steel until he reached its resolution with a more minimalist sweep and a lighter feel (fig. 1.99d). As Aaron Betsky has written of the chair:

This composition reduces the material to a minimum, while giving the body the sense that the piece is molding itself to one's weight and shape. It also makes the whole piece appear as if it were about to leap off the floor. By honing the details so that the connections between the various pieces are almost invisible, Tuttle draws the eye to the lines of the chair. Yet he does not hide the construction of his pieces. One can understand the relationship between tension and compression, between support and cantilever, in every piece he makes.[65]

Tuttle was by no means limited to a preoccupation with a series of design challenges that he resolved through a sequence of evolutions or iterations. He also played with various other possibilities in form and structure, adapting elements of his own design vocabulary, sometimes reaching back to very early designs that he sought to improve either visually or functionally. For example, he experimented with various configurations of tubular steel bases that supported seats and backs made of molded wood (fig. 1.101). " Fat Tube" Chair (1996; fig. 1.102) continued Tuttle's experimentation with factory-made plywood cylinders of varying diameters.[66] Using this material allowed him to readily incorporate the circle, a geometric form he long favored for its clarity and sensuousness.

This chair cleverly incorporates the maple-veneered cylinder as a part of the base, while the upholstered seat and back are supported and stabilized by a striking arrangement of penetrating steel elements. His Laminated Low Chair (2000; fig. 1.103) also incorporates the circle as a key design element at the same time it intentionally improves upon the early Laminata Chair of 1977 produced by Strässle (see fig. 2.22).

As is abundantly evident, much of his furniture has a distinctive quirky playfulness. Even in chairs as fundamentally elegant as the "Z" Chair, there is an evocative liveliness. Periodically he designed another "folly" piece that was purposefully humorous. Tuttle's Folly (1990; fig. 1.104) is just such a piece, designed to function in part as a chair and in part as a silent valet. There is an uncanny relationship between Tuttle's Folly and Coop Himmelblau's Vodöl Chair of 1989 (fig. 1.105), produced by Vitra AG in Basel. In both, upholstered seats rest precariously on a length of I-beam; both are predominantly a cool blue and white. However, Coop Himmelblau's subversive deconstruction of earlier chairs by Le Corbusier and Mies van der Rohe is clearly different in intent from the lightheartedness of Tuttle's Folly, evident in Tuttle's use of "ticking" upholstery (which he had used earlier in the Landes line of 1970) and the "cracked" disk supporting the chair. Both his Baby Folly (1995; fig. 1.106) and the Comic Chair (2001; fig. 1.107) are pure fun in their combination of colors, shapes, and materials.

A furniture type that fascinated Tuttle in terms of the relationships that existed between its form, material, and function was the easel. He began exploring the easel in the 1960s, looking for a way to design a support that would minimally interfere with the appreciation of the art displayed on it. He developed a prototype in 1986 for Strässle that combined a tall cylinder of walnut with an adjustable walnut and black-painted steel shelf (fig. 1.108a). Although

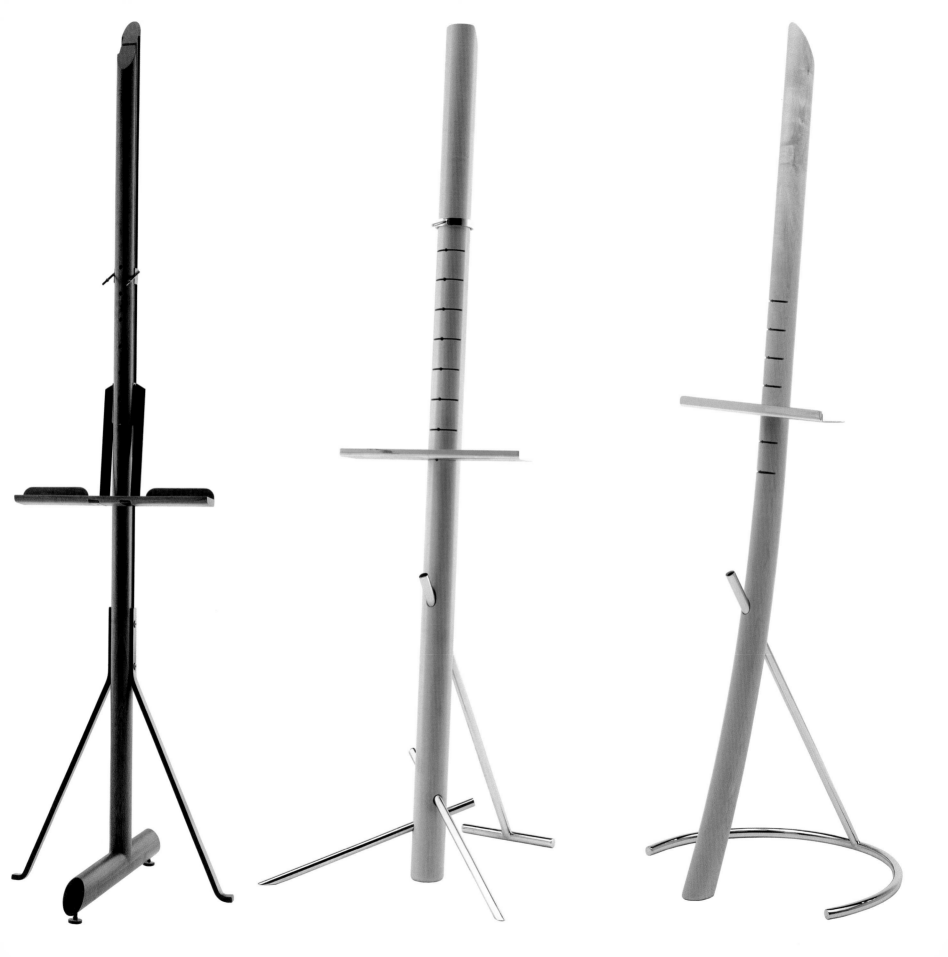

1.108a–c Easel Evolution
(opposite, left to right):

(A) 1986
Walnut, powder-coated steel
Produced by Bud Tullis, Solvang, California
Collection of Cliff and Mandy Einstein

(B) 1991
Maple, chrome-plated steel
Produced by Bud Tullis, Solvang, California
Collection of Carol L. Valentine

(C) 1995
Maple, chrome-plated steel
Produced by Bud Tullis, Solvang, California
Collection of Eli and Leatrice Luria

1.109 (Top) **Bench**, 2000
Maple, cherry
Produced by Bud Tullis, Solvang, California
Collection of the University Art Museum,
UCSB, Architecture and Design Collection

1.110 (Bottom) **Behind-the-Sofa Table**, 1995
Maple, polished, brass-tined aluminium
Produced by Bud Tullis, Solvang, California
Collection of the Duca Family

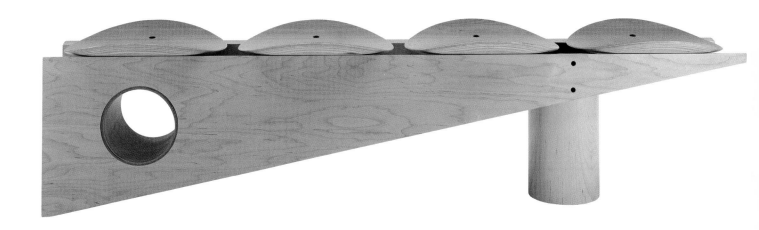

this design was never put into production, several years later he made two design modifications to achieve a "cleaner," simpler form using a wider cylinder of maple and contrasting chromed steel (figs. 1.108b, c). The 1995 version reduces the complexity of the easel's tubular steel base structure and introduces a subtle but graceful curve to the upright maple cylinder.

As has been noted, Tuttle produced many unique exploratory pieces, as well as works done on client request, for residential and contract purposes.[67] Dining tables were among the most popular of his private commissions along with related sideboards, buffets, benches, bookshelves and behind-the-sofa tables (figs. 1.109, 1.110, 1.112–1.115). Continuing the tradition he began in Basel with the Doetsch, Grether & Cie. headquarters, he designed a number of complete office interiors in Santa Barbara, where he combined unique pieces (especially desks, shelving, and conference tables) with manufactured seating by Strässle (see fig. 1.56). The same is true of private residences, where he designed all the furnishings for one or more rooms (fig. 1.116) or was involved in home remodels that incorporate space renovations/expansions with built-in and custom-designed furniture (figs. 1.117, 1.118).

Tuttle also completed several projects that involved problem solving in a larger design context. In 1994 he partnered with landscape architect Isabelle Greene to undertake the landscape renovation of a seven-acre estate in Carpinteria, embarking on his first landscape exploration.[68] Tuttle designed boldly colored, slightly bowed freestanding walls to provide definition to the site and lead visitors to the house's main entry, which formerly had been difficult to find (p. 186). Greene developed the landscaping plan, including soft fields of drought-tolerant plants that function as a fitting contrast to Tuttle's minimalist but dramatic walls. The effectiveness of the Tuttle-Greene partnership is especially evident in the three-foot wide circular aperture in one wall that beautifully draws the eye to the plantings beyond.

CULMINATING MOMENTS

After 1996, Paul Tuttle completed some of his most important designs, achieving the "essence" he had long sought in concept and material. There are a number of recent pieces that Tuttle identified as culminations of ideas, wherein he resolved problems of structure, form, line, material, and detail (or lack thereof): "For me, it is about getting absolutely to the truth, a bare minimum, where there is just no excess at all."[69] Tuttle's insistence on taking his designs to what he called their essence comes in part from the early and enduring influence of Alvin Lustig. His evolutions were quests for solutions and in their finality became what Tuttle identified as "essence" pieces. The Super "Z" Chair of 1996, for example, resolved an idea Tuttle began exploring in 1964; its striking linear composition in stainless steel is an exquisite complement to the wooden seat and back (fig. 1.111). The final three-legged chair in Tuttle's design evolution, which began with his Anaconda of 1970/71, is the Spencer Chair of 1999 (fig. 1.119). Asked why this chair represents the essence of that particular design evolution, Tuttle explained:

I think just because of the length of time which has been spent in the exploration of this chair as an idea. The three-legged chair is a perfect illustration of one where I never really felt that I had solved the problem of connecting wood to metal and feeling secure with it—that it is really able to take all kinds of punishment because of the instability of wood and its movement in relationship to metal. In this chair, that has been solved. And solved so that there is no way in the world you can separate the metal piece from the wood piece. And it is done in a way that creates its own ornamentation. With the inset of the metal piece, it's anchored.[70]

1.111 Super "Z" Chair, 1996
Cherry, stainless steel
Produced by Bud Tullis, Solvang;
steel fabrication by Spike Pollorena,
Paradise Mobile Welding,
Santa Barbara, California
Collection of Joan and Bill Crawford

1.112 (Opposite) Interior view of Berkus
Art Box, Santa Barbara, California, 1986
Art Bench, 1986
Walnut, cherry, koa, painted tubular steel
Produced by Bud Tullis, Solvang, California
Collection of Barry Berkus

1.113 (Top) Investment Group
of Santa Barbara conference room, 1996
Buffet by Paul Tuttle, 1996
Walnut, granite
Produced by Bud Tullis, Solvang, California

1.114 (Bottom) Living room display wall
in private residence, 2001
Wall unit by Paul Tuttle, 1995
Oak. Produced by Julie Stark,
Santa Barbara, California
"Fat Tube" Chair by Paul Tuttle
(see fig. 1.102)

1.115a, b Study in Assassi residence,
Santa Barbara, California, 2001
Dining table by Paul Tuttle, 1989 (see fig. 1.92)
Skate dining chairs by Paul Tuttle, 1993
produced by Strässle International

1.116 Dining room in Tuttle residence,
Santa Barbara, California, 2001
Laminated Low Chair by Paul Tuttle
(see fig. 1.103), 2000
The Spencer Chair by Paul Tuttle
(see fig. 1.119), 1999
Cylinder dining table by Paul Tuttle
Produced by Bud Tullis, Solvang,
California, 1999

1.117 Upstairs office in the Andina residence,
Santa Barbara, California, 1998
Desk by Paul Tuttle, 1997
Maple, painted wood
Produced by Bud Tullis, Solvang, California,
Skate Dining Chair by Paul Tuttle (see fig. 1.68), 1993
Produced by Strässle International

1.118 Entry in the Andina residence,
Santa Barbara, California, 1998
Bookshelves by Paul Tuttle, 1997
Walnut, maple
Produced by Bud Tullis, Solvang, California

The Spencer Chair borrows design elements from Tuttle's "66" Series, especially the distinctive flaring leg and angular armrest of his "66/95" chair. The steel brace under the seat is also a direct borrowing, but here, as Tuttle says, he has structurally and aesthetically joined the metal and wood in a highly successful result.

Tuttle considered his Arco Chair of 1976 (see fig. 1.54) his first essential piece and his best Strässle design:

Well, the Arco chair is the best thing I've done here by far.... that chair is probably the only chair that I've ever done which I think is an essence piece, except maybe this new one I'm trying to do now [the Profile Chair]. There are so few pieces to that chair yet it still comes out with a certain kind of sensitivity in relation to proportion, in relationship to the round form, and the sense of flexibility in the strap form.

I was really and truly striving for the simplest thing possible where I felt it came out of an honest to God idea.... It is one of those things that came as close to really being a pure kind of a thought.[71]

In 1980 Tuttle designed a wood and cane version, called Arco II, which made use of the same elegant arcs of strap steel but eliminated the leather upholstery. Although when it was first designed Tuttle had hoped that Strässle would put it into production, it exists today only in custom versions. He returned to the same design in 1997 (see fig. 2.31), with slight modifications to the width and height of the seat. The wood and cane bring to the chair the warmth Tuttle preferred, and also provide an opportunity to showcase its beautiful handcrafted details.

In 1998 Paul Tuttle had what he considered a breakthrough with the design of the Profile Chair (fig. 1.120), as he explained:

Because there is almost nothing there. I mean it's an absolutely minimalist piece. I did little things there that would be diametrically opposed to what would be my natural thinking as a person interested in structure in the sense that the way that chair comes down, and the seat, the piece comes in here [supporting the seat], the other piece [supporting the base] drops down here.... All of these things became a part of that one single curved piece of strap metal.... And its being curved that way was diametrically opposed to these rigid pieces [the steel elements that intersect it] but somehow when I look at it, this all works. And the reason I'm convinced that it works—this is ironic—is that I've seen this happen in trees. In other words, I can point to a tree right out there where the branch's relationship coming off the trunk into another branch works because it happens with a space between them.[72]

The Profile Chair continued Tuttle's adaptation of the cantilever to a chair. What is utterly new is the single strong gesture of the strap steel in profile, which has given the chair its name. The beautiful curves in the molded seat and back are intended to comfortably receive the body, with their alignment encouraging the weight of a person be borne far back in the seat. Whereas the lines of the strap steel create a strong compositional statement, so too do the wood forms. In the same way that Tuttle describes the steel elements as "branching" off the central steel curve, the laminated wood forms of the chair's seat and back evoke the distinctive shape of a tulip petal. The luster and beautiful grain patterns in the wood contrast elegantly with the chromed steel in an aesthetic that typifies the best of Tuttle's designs.

1.119 (Top) **The Spencer Chair**, 1999
Mahogany, painted steel
Produced by Bud Tullis, Solvang, California
Private Collection

1.120 (Bottom) **Profile Chair**, 2000
Walnut, chrome-plated stainless steel
Produced by Bud Tullis, Solvang, California
and Spike Pollorena, Paradise Mobile
Welding, Santa Barbara, California
Private Collection

1.121 Lounge III, 2000
Plywood, cherry, painted steel, leather
Produced by Bud Tullis, Solvang, California,
and Spike Pollorena, Paradise Mobile
Welding, Santa Barbara, California
Collection of Carey Berkus

1.122 Pisces III Coffee Table, 1997
Appleply, glass
Produced by Bud Tullis, Solvang, California
Collection of the University Art Museum,
UCSB, Gift of Suzanne Duca

Inarguably, the Super "Z" Chair, the Arco Chair and the Profile Chair are Tuttle's quintessential designs. In all three, the manipulation of wood showcases its natural beauty and reveals a preference for the handcrafted. Steel, Tuttle's nod to the machine, provides his designs with structural strength and dominates the visual composition with powerful lines.

Not satisfied with a concentration on these key design challenges, Tuttle produced several other pieces in the late 1990s that also represent culminations of particular design explorations. His Lounge III of 1999/2000 (fig. 1.121) continued the thinking evident in his earlier pieces but reached a material and structural solution that suited Tuttle's preferences. The laminated plywood base provides strength but has a lightness of appearance that makes the reclining surface appear to float. The use of heavy natural-colored leather gives the recliner both suppleness and comfort; its steel frame supplies the necessary support and also allows the back to be raised or lowered. As an overall design statement, this piece is focused around one strong structural gesture but reveals the beauty in the contrasting materials and in the complexity of details.

Another late work, the Pisces III Coffee Table (1997; fig. 1.122) epitomizes Paul Tuttle's idea of an essence piece: it reduces the materials and forms to a bare minimum yet does so with a distinctive sophistication. There is a purity and delicacy to this piece that belies its intended functionality—it is much more seductive as something to look at than as something to use. It is hard to imagine interrupting the cleanliness of this table's pure forms by placing anything upon it.

Tuttle claimed not to have had a single design philosophy, even though it is clear from the examples discussed above that seeking an essence was central to his approach.

His long career was concerned with meeting this challenge and doing so with work that was authentic and inventive. He was his own harshest judge of when his work had met these expectations, and he rarely settled for easy solutions, preferring to seek something uniquely his own:

Well, first of all, I have to say in all sincerity, I have never had any goal, as such, for any of my work. My interest and concern has always been with the spirit of the thing and the integrity of it. And I, at least in my sense of it, never associated that with a goal. It had to do with an inner thing that I feel. For myself, I associate "soul" with certain pieces, even though I don't think that the word is right because I don't see soul in the context of a material thing of this kind—a piece of applied art. But I have always felt there is something in there above and beyond what has to do with design—a little bit of a sense of mystery that one could not put their finger on. And part of that came out of my having this intense feeling, and I don't know why it was, but I sure had it and have to this day, that I did not want my work to be like anyone else's work. I have no objectivity about how good or bad it would be, but I did about it having it's own unique quality.[73]

Paul Tuttle's last designs sustain the originality evident in his earliest pieces. In the fifty-year retrospective exhibition held at the University Art Museum at the University of California, Santa Barbara, in 2001/2002, the presentation of his first designs alongside those most recently done completed the cycle of his career (see p.185).[74] For Tuttle, this event "closed the circle" and confirmed that his final pieces really did take his designs as far as he could go.[75] It is a tribute to his integrity, authenticity, and untiring sense of joy that he spent a lifetime striving for these culminating moments and in so doing avoided the temptation to succumb to the changing trends of late-twentieth-century consumerism.

1.123 Paul Tuttle, 2001.

When you asked me earlier about what I felt
I had achieved, the thing I feel in the recent pieces
is the spirit and soul of whatever I'm about
as a human being. I couldn't care less how they
are interpreted from a critic's point of view
or in relationship to other things. I think they have
a spirit to them, and I think it comes out of my
own being. And that's the prime essence for me.[76]
Paul Tuttle, 2001

NOTES

Unless otherwise noted, all interviews were conducted by the author in Santa Barbara, California

1 Paul Tuttle quoted in Steven Frank, "Playful Ingenuity," *Metropolis* 12 (March 1993): 47.

2 Dennis Sharp, *The Illustrated Encyclopedia of Architects and Architecture* (New York: Quatro Publishing, 1991), 102–103.

3 For more on Alvin Lustig, see the essay by Kurt Helfrich that appears as chapter 3 in this volume.

4 Interview with Paul Tuttle, October 1997.

5 Interview with Paul Tuttle, October 1997.

6 Tuttle learned this years later when he returned to Taliesin and visited the man who ran the wood shop. Unfortunately, the design is now lost.

7 See Frank "Playful Ingenuity," 61. The *Good Design* exhibition program began as a partnership between the Museum of Modern Art in New York City and the Merchandise Mart in Chicago and represented the first collaboration between an art museum and a wholesale merchandising center. The Eames office designed the inaugural exhibition in 1950 and successive exhibitions were executed by different designers. The aim of the exhibition series was to present "the best new examples in modern design in home furnishings." See John Neuhart, Marilyn Neuhart, and Ray Eames, *Eames Design: The Work of the Office of Charles and Ray Eames* (New York: Harry N. Abrams, Inc., 1989), 130–131. The Eames office included a slide of Tuttle's table in one of Charles's lectures. Although Charles certainly noted the distinctiveness of Tuttle's work, many biographical sketches erroneously identify Eames as having selected Tuttle's table for the 1951 *Good Design* exhibition.

8 Paul Tuttle quoted in Beverly Johnson, "The Designer Speaks," *Los Angeles Times* (December 4, 1966).

9 Interview with Thornton Ladd, Ojai, California, July 2001.

10 Interview with Paul Tuttle, October 1997.

11 Interview with Paul Tuttle, October 1997.

12 Interview with Paul Tuttle, Gstaad, Switzerland, June 1997. Also quoted in Hunter Drohojowska, "Design Dialogue: Paul Tuttle," *Architectural Digest* (February 1990): 130.

13 Paul Tuttle quoted in Frank, "Playful Ingenuity."

14 Interview with Paul Tuttle, May 2001.

15 Interview with Paul Tuttle, April 2001.

16 See Pasadena Art Museum, *California Design/8* (Pasadena: Pasadena Art Museum, 1962). The pieces by Tuttle included in this exhibition were: an eight-foot-long laminated wood table top with an easel-like frame to adjust the height (1961); a walnut shell hung on a stainless steel frame to support a leather seat based on the seat of a sports car (1959); and versions of the Adjustable Table of 1962, Dining Chair of 1959 (with cane upholstery), and Inverted "Y" Lounge Chair of 1960 (with raw silk upholstery), made to be sold in the Tucker Shops in Santa Barbara.

17 Interview with Eudorah Moore, July 2001.

18 Eudorah Moore, *The Furniture Designs of Paul Tuttle* (Pasadena: Pasadena Art Museum, 1967).

19 See the essay by Kurt Helfrich that appears as chapter 3 in this volume.

20 Interview with Paul Tuttle, May 1997.

21 Henry J. Seldis, "A Beach Pavilion," *Art in America* 49, no.2 (1961): 78. This Tuttle design is described as "one of the most beautiful and finest quality houses of this style in the area [Montecito]" in the important volume by Herb Andree and Noel Young, *Santa Barbara Architecture: From Spanish Colonial to Modern* (Santa Barbara, Capra Press, 1975), 231.

22 Interview with Paul Tuttle, October 1997. Unfortunately, the photographs of the Taliesin tent design were destroyed.

23 Letter written by George Dangerfield, November 1961, Architecture and Design Collection, University Art Museum, UCSB.

24 Paul Tuttle moved out of this house around 1995 after the Dangerfield children sold the property.

25 See Dan MacMasters, "Mesa Magic by Paul Tuttle," *Los Angeles Times* (January 15, 1978) and Frank's "Playful Ingenuity." Tuttle's friend the architect Andy Neumann told me that the house allowed such a strong sense of the surrounding environment to come inside that one felt liberated, despite its small size. He, like many others who visited Paul at home, left wishing he could live there.

26 Esther Grether, who became head of Doetsch, Grether after the death of her husband, Hans, recently moved this furniture to another factory space in Basel that has been converted into her home. She continued to be a major patron of Paul Tuttle's work, which she commissioned over the years for her corporate offices and her personal residence.

27 This new corporate conference room replaced the one on the sixth floor, which is now used largely for private meetings and gatherings.

28 Interview with Paul Tuttle, Basel, Switzerland, June 1997.

29 Ibid.

30 It was Doris Dietschi, an interior designer at Hofstetters of Basel, who suggested to Alex Strässle that he meet Paul Tuttle. Tuttle did some work for Hofstetters in connection with Doetsch, Grether.

31 Interview with Maria Strässle, Kirchberg, Switzerland, June 1997.

32 Cara Greenberg, *Op to Pop: Furniture of the 1960s* (Boston: Bulfinch Press, Little, Brown and Company, 1999), 18–19.

33 According to Tuttle, this chair, upholstered in fabric, was originally made by Globus and sold for $99. Interview with Paul Tuttle, May 2001.

34 Interview with Paul Tuttle, May 2001.

35 See David A. Hanks, *Innovative Furniture in America from 1800 to the Present* (New York: Horizon Press, 1981, 120.

36 Unfortunately, the original molds Tuttle carved by hand were destroyed when the second chair was produced. In Tuttle's absence (he had returned to California), Strässle redid the forms but without the subtle detailing Tuttle had added, especially in the definition of the edges. Tuttle never

felt satisfied with the way the self-skinning surface was intended to "look" like leather when it was not. Despite its commercial success for Strässle, the chair lacks the "truth in materials" that was so important to Tuttle and to the modernist credo.

37 Hanks, *Innovative Furniture*, 119–120. The Leonardo Collection was first introduced in the United States in June 1980 at the Merchandise Mart in Chicago.

38 See Cara Greenberg, *Mid-Century Modern: Furniture of the 1950s* (New York: Harmony Books, 1984), 14–16.

39 Interview with Paul Tuttle, Kirchberg, Switzerland, June 1997.

40 This quotation appears in a page taken from a journal and retained by Paul Tuttle. Tuttle meticulously trimmed such reviews, and unfortunately in doing so removed identification of the source.

41 See "Noted Designer to appear in L.A. Symposium," in *Santa Barbara News Press* (March 15, 1981).

42 Kirk Von Blunck, " An Experiment of Ideas: Paul Tuttle," *Iowa Architect* (winter 1989): 8.

43 It is unfortunate that Landes was not successful with this line, which was only produced for a short time.

44 The Youmans had a gallery in La Jolla. Tuttle visited the gallery because it represented the artist George Ball. Scott Youmans is an architect and Valerie is an interior designer. Interview with Paul Tuttle, June 1998.

45 Helen Barnes, "La Haute Grange: On an Alpine Slope near the Village of Gstaad," *Architectural Digest* 37, pt. 3 (December 1980): 74.

46 See William Weaver, "Switzerland's La Cour de Ferme: Restoring a Seventeenth-Century Chalet near Gstaad," *Architectural Digest* 47, no. 22, (October 1990): 256–263, 294.

47 Interview with Paul Tuttle, Kirchberg, Switzerland, June 1997. Today, the Skate Series is being produced by Strässle International and is distributed through Janus et Cie in Los Angeles.

48 See *Paul Tuttle Designer* (Santa Barbara: Santa Barbara Museum of Art, 1978) with an introduction by Eudorah Moore.

49 MacMasters, "Mesa Magic by Paul Tuttle."

50 Paul Tuttle quoted in Angeline Vogl, "Paul Tuttle at Play," *Designers West* (February 1993): 6.

51 Interview with Paul Tuttle, October 1997.

52 Interview with Paul Tuttle, April 2001.

53 See Aaron Betsky "Still Modern after All These Years: The Work of Paul Tuttle in Context," *Paul Tuttle: 3 Evolutions +* (Santa Barbara: Santa Barbara Contemporary Arts Forum, 1995).

54 "Paul Tuttle, An Interview," *Designers West* (February 1974): 82–83.

55 Interview with Paul Tuttle, April 2001.

56 Valerie Havas, "Paul Tuttle's Furniture with 10-speeds," *Santa Barbara Independent* (June 1983).

57 Ibid.

58 Ibid.

59 Tuttle quoted in Drohojowska, "Design Dialogue: Paul Tuttle," 122.

60 Tuttle was very self-conscious about his ability to draw and the quality of his drawings. Although he agonized over his drawings, they are in fact quite beautiful. He used a minimum of lines to communicate what was needed to build his pieces. One of the hallmarks of the Tuttle-Tullis partnership was Tullis's ability to read Tuttle's drawings. Because Tuttle considered his drawings purely functional, many were destroyed once a piece was produced. Fortunately, a number of drawings of key pieces were kept and are now a part of the Architecture and Design Collection, University Art Museum, UCSB.

61 Strictly speaking, the beginning of the three-legged chair evolution is 1970/71 with the Anaconda Chair designed for Strässle (see fig. 1.47)

62 Interview with Paul Tuttle, April 2001.

63 Interview with Bud Tullis, July 2001.

64 A production model of the "Z" Chair, based on the 1996 version, is currently under development by Forms and Surfaces, Carpinteria, California. This distinctive contemporary chair is intended for a contract market.

65 See Aaron Betsky, "Still Modern after All These Years: The Work of Paul Tuttle in Context," in *Paul Tuttle: 3 Evolutions +*, 6.

66 This chair was put into limited production by the Summit Design Studio in 1998 under the name, The Cylinder Collection. Tuttle designed a "Side Table" to go with "The Cylinder Chair." The designs were advertised in a product catalog published by Summit, which at the time had a showroom in the Pacific Design Center, Los Angeles.

67 With the exception of the sofa-benches he designed for Strässle International, the one type of furniture Tuttle seems not to have designed is the sofa.

68 See Michael Leccese, "Opposites Attract," *Landscape Architecture* 86 (May 1996): 30–37.

69 Quoted in Frank, "Playful Ingenuity," *Metropolis*, 63.

70 Interview with Paul Tuttle, April 2001.

71 Interview with Paul Tuttle, Kirchberg, Switzerland, June 1997.

72 Interview with Paul Tuttle, May 2001.

73 Interview with Paul Tuttle, April 2001.

74 See the exhibition brochure: Marla C. Berns, *Paul Tuttle Designs* (Santa Barbara: University Art Museum, UCSB), 2001.

75 Conversation with Paul Tuttle, June 2002.

76 Interview with Paul Tuttle, April 2001.

Cosmopolitan Conversations:
The Furniture Designs of Paul Tuttle

MICHAEL DARLING

It is tempting to write modern design history in terms resembling the big bang theory, with undisputed masterpieces exploding onto the scene from the ethers of individual creativity. Very few objects, however, come into being through creative technological musings with little or no connection to prior conventions. Most works of design emerge from a lineage of point and counterpoint that carries forth older traditions while simultaneously breaking ground for new modes of expression. One has only to think of seminal works such as Mies van der Rohe's Barcelona Chair (1929; fig. 2.2), the lines of which owe a debt to the ancient Greek Klismos Chair, or the progression from Gerrit Rietveld's cantilevered Zig-Zag Chair (1932–1934; fig. 2.3) to Verner Panton's fiberglass Stacking Chair (1960; fig. 2.4) and on to numerous subsequent iterations in order to find a more accurate picture of how the history of design is written.

Paul Tuttle's work clearly demonstrates this tendency. Throughout his long and productive career, he actively engaged the history of design in his work, constantly questioning what makes a chair a chair or a table a table, while at the same time unapologetically orienting his creations to the here and now. While one can often detect references to other objects in his designs, there is always an accompanying "countermove," as if he were engaged in a spirited dialogue or an intense chess match with the whole world of things. This competitive spirit resulted in a fascinating body of work distinguished by technical innovation, exquisite taste, a fluent grasp of current design discourse, and perhaps most important, an overriding sense of humor. Tuttle's oeuvre can be seen as a witty and cosmopolitan conversation with the world of design, a dialogue in which admirers of his chairs are invited to participate.

2.1 (Opposite) Paul Tuttle
at the Design Source,
Santa Barbara, California, 1989

2.2 Ludwig **Mies van der Rohe** (1886–1969)
MR 90 Chair (Barcelona Chair), 1929
Chrome-plated steel, leather
Produced by Berliner Metallgewerbe
Josef Müller, Berlin
Vitra Design Museum, Weil am Rhein

2.3 Gerrit Thomas **Rietveld** (1888–1964)
Zig-Zag Chair, 1932–1934
Stained elm, brass
Produced by Metz & Co., Amsterdam
Vitra Design Museum, Weil am Rhein

2.4 Verner **Panton** (1926–1998)
Stacking Chair, 1960
First version: Varnished high-resistance foam
Herman Miller AG, Zeeland, Michigan
Philadelphia Museum of Art: Purchased
with funds contributed by Mr. and Mrs. John
W. Drayton, 1973, acc. no 73-95-1

2.5 (Left) **Armchair**, 1952
Walnut, metal, wool upholstery
Produced by John Van Breda,
Pasadena, California
Santa Barbara Museum of Art,
Gift of Barbara C. Wallace in memory
of Esther Bear and Mary O. Steel

2.6 Finn **Juhl** (1912–1989)
Armchair, 1951
Teak and leather upholstery
Baker Furniture, Grand Rapids, Michigan
Philadelphia Museum of Art:
Gift of Mr. and Mrs. N. Richard Miller,
1980, acc. no 1980-138-1

The currency of Tuttle's taste was evident in his very first forays into furniture design. The Elliptical Coffee Table of 1950 (see fig. 1.4), with its tapered legs, delicate interpenetrating crossbeams, and visible joinery, was selected for inclusion in the 1951 *Good Design* exhibition. Co-organized by the Museum of Modern Art in New York and the Chicago Merchandise Mart, this yearly exhibition was a way for the museum to proselytize concerning the virtues of modern design, and its track record for choosing the best objects of the day was unsurpassed. Tuttle's table was selected by guest juror Finn Juhl, one of the foremost designers of the period. Juhl's own work of this time bore a strong affinity to that of Tuttle. Like Tuttle, Juhl favored the rich color and silky finish of walnut, and his preference for precision craftsmanship and organic forms is echoed in the Tuttle coffee table. And yet there is a difference. Tuttle's subtle flaunting of convention by floating the short crossmember of the table's leg structure through a hole in the longer dowel slyly subverts structural integrity and brazenly pushes the table toward sculpture. The deviation from established norms and an attraction to sculptural pizzazz would characterize most of Tuttle's later work, but it is surprising to find them so early in his development as a designer.

Tuttle's Armchair of 1952 (fig. 2.5) could also easily have won praise from Juhl, for its orchestration of distinct but interconnecting parts is reminiscent of the elder designer's style. The thin upholstered seat—floating apart from the structural skeleton of gracefully turned wood arms and legs—announces the chair's three-dimensionality. It is an object that traces, rather than takes up, space in a room. The irregular shape of the upholstered back piece, which is ergonomically designed to cradle the shoulders and accommodate the lower back at the same time, is the sort of abstract form that Juhl also employed on many occasions (fig. 2.6). In the postwar years, Danish designers like Juhl ushered in a craze for their clean-lined, wholesome designs in hardwoods, such as walnut and teak. They rarely mixed contrasting materials, and when wood was called for, it was mostly paired with other natural surfaces like leather, wool, rattan, or woven jute. Through such preferences, these designers strove for an organic connection to the earth, whereas subtle details in the Tuttle chair suggest other motives. The shiny metal slugs that separate the wood legs from the floor serve as witty pedestals, raising Tuttle's creation off the ground and singling it out as a highly aesthetic, urbane object, as opposed to a woodsy evocation of nature. Such "prosthetic" devices would reoccur throughout the course of Tuttle's work, mischievously tweaking the form language of other designers.

From the late 1940s to the mid-1950s Tuttle, who was based in Los Angeles, came into direct contact with a number of sophisticated mentors, including Frank Lloyd Wright, Alvin Lustig, and Thornton Ladd, and was exposed to a range of cutting-edge cultural opportunities. Los Angeles at this time was blossoming into a mecca for advanced architectural experimentation, and its art scene was likewise beginning to come into its own. In 1956 Tuttle moved to Santa Barbara—then still a sleepy resort community—but this relocation did not result in any easing of his artistic curiosity or ambition and, on the contrary, saw Tuttle expand into private architectural practice and an even greater devotion to design work. His stunning Dangerfield beach house of 1959 (see figs. 1.24, 3.12) was the equal of any of the refined post-and-beam architecture then sprouting up around Southern California, and the furniture he began to undertake at this time was similarly adventurous.

2.7 Dining Chair, 1959
Maple, linen upholstery
Produced by Stanley Reifel,
Carpinteria, California
Collection of University Art
Museum, UCSB, Purchase
by Friends of Paul Tuttle Fund

The dining chairs Tuttle created for the beach house (fig. 2.7) were superficially conventional, resembling other chairs like those by George Nelson (fig. 2.10) or Franco Albini (fig. 2.8) until one closely inspected their details and proportions. The chairs by both contemporaries are rather straightforward, utilitarian designs. Tuttle's by contrast is sprightly, allusive, and delicate, inviting the beholder to scrutinize the way it is put together and the relationships of the parts to the whole. The L-shaped back and seat, for instance, levitate above the leg structure and away from the enveloping arms. The joinery between the undercarriage of the seat and the tapering legs is both a brilliant piece of woodworking and an unabashedly modernist exposure of tectonic parts. The seat back is slightly taller and more slender than that of most chairs of its kind, and the seat protrudes a little further than expected from its base, distinguishing it even more from its brethren in the furniture world, while giving it a tautness and leanness that invites zoomorphic comparisons. The gentle outward curve at the tips of the legs is likewise almost animalistic, suggesting a gazelle poised to jump. In this way, the chair is perhaps best compared to the work of Carlo Mollino, whose sensual, idiosyncratic furniture also alluded to living, breathing, bodies in motion (fig. 2.9). Like Mollino, Tuttle often worked on custom orders, bypassing the sort of standardizing that mass manufacture requires and allowing an attention to (and even fetishization of) detail that was impossible in chairs such as those of Nelson and Albini.

2.8 Franco **Albini** (1905–1977)
Armchair, 1948
Wood
Produced by Knoll International,
Inc., New York

2.9 Carlo **Mollino** (1905–1973)
Casa Cattaneo Chair, 1953
Bent plywood, brass
Produced by Apelli & Varesio, Turin, Italy
Vitra Design Museum, Weil am Rhein

2.10 George **Nelson** (1908–1986)
4663 Dining Chair, 1946
Walnut, upholstery
Produced by Herman Miller, Zeeland,
Michigan

2.11 Double Cane Tub Chair, 1965
Walnut, cane
Produced by John Van Breda,
Pasadena, California
Collection of Joan and Jim Tanner

Other Tuttle creations of the period also illustrate the designer manipulating the constituent parts of what appear to be rather normal chairs or tables to such a degree that the ordinary suddenly becomes extraordinary. His Pony Chair of 1961, Writing Table of 1962, and Double Cane Tub Chair of 1965 (fig. 2.11) are excellent examples of such canny reworkings of mundane furniture types. A similar reassessment of historical forms is found in the works of all the giants of modern furniture design, from Mies to Le Corbusier, Charlotte Perriand, Marcel Breuer, and Gio Ponti (fig. 2.12), and became a staple of the so-called postmodernists who even more openly acknowledged their sources. Robert Venturi (fig. 2.13), Alessandro Mendini, Archizoom, and Coop Himmelblau have all made signature furniture works that both recall and refute their lineage.

Generationally and aesthetically (if not ideologically), Tuttle hovers in between these two eras. He entered the profession during the postwar height of the modern movement and embraced many of its concerns for advanced engineering and truthful expression of materials, but his career really gained momentum in the 1960s when modernism began to lose its sway with young designers and a more irreverent, even iconoclastic attitude prevailed. As we have come to understand with a little historical distance, these distinctions are often hard to maintain, and to paraphrase Venturi, Tuttle could perhaps be seen as a "both-and" designer rather than an exclusionary "either-or" one, maintaining a modernist sensibility when it comes to construction and materials and a postmodernist whimsy in his forms and intent.

2.12 Gio (Giovanni) **Ponti** (1891–1979)
Superleggera Chair, 1957
Painted ash, cane
Produced by Figli di Amedeo Cassina,
Meda (near Milan)
Vitra Design Museum, Weil am Rhein

2.13 Robert **Venturi** (b. 1925)
Queen Anne Chair, 1984
Molded multiplex, laminated
plastic, imitation leather
Produced by Knoll International,
Inc., New York
Vitra Design Museum, Weil am Rhein

2.14 Field Officer's Chair, 1964
Wood, metal, leather
Produced by Swenson & Peterson,
Pasadena, California
Collection of Nancy and Jesse Alexander

In the 1960s, Tuttle embarked on some of his most aggressive interventions vis-à-vis the history of design—his cosmopolitan conversations turning into sly interrogations of his interlocutors. In a design such as the Field Officer's Chair of 1964 (fig. 2.14), for instance, he seems almost to be forcing Le Corbusier and Marcel Breuer to "come clean" in terms of their indebtedness to vernacular designs. These designers created iconic chrome and leather chairs in the 1920s that fit perfectly with the "machine for living" aesthetic of avant-garde modern design—Le Corbusier with the Basculant Chair that he designed with Pierre Jeanneret and Charlotte Perriand in 1928 (fig. 2.15) and Breuer with his much-copied Wassily Chair of 1925 (fig. 2.16)—but both chairs trace their roots back to casual, lightweight examples used by the military. To be sure, they were extremely radical statements for their day, bringing industrial production and abstract compositional ideas into the domestic sphere, but by the 1960s they were also iconic targets for reappraisal. In his Field Officer's Chair, Tuttle seems to offer an abstract demonstration of how a chair works. The painted metal parts provide a cool, rational framework in which Old World materials such as wood and leather can do their jobs. These venerable materials perform their functions—the wood as legs and the leather as seat, arm, and back supports—but it is really the connecting metal armature that holds everything together. Like contemporary artist Charles Ray's sculpture *How a Table Works* (1986; fig. 2.17), Tuttle's chair is an utterly conceptual object involved as much with critiquing and commenting on conventions of use and construction as it is with the sculptural presence of objects in space.

2.15 Le Corbusier (1887–1965),
Pierre **Jeanneret** (1896–1967),
and Charlotte **Perriand** (b. 1903)
Basculant Chair, 1928
Chrome-plated tubular steel, leather, steel springs
Produced by the designers
Vitra Design Museum, Weil am Rhein

2.16 Marcel **Breuer** (1902–1981)
Wassily Chair, 1925
Cold bent, nickel-plated tubular steel, fabric
Produced by Standard Möbel Lengyel & Co., Berlin
Vitra Design Museum, Weil am Rhein

2.17 Charles **Ray** (b. 1953)
How a Table Works, 1986
Steel with metal box, thermos, plastic cup, terracotta pot with synthetic plant, painted metal can
The Museum of Contemporary Art, Los Angeles;
Gift of Lannan Foundation

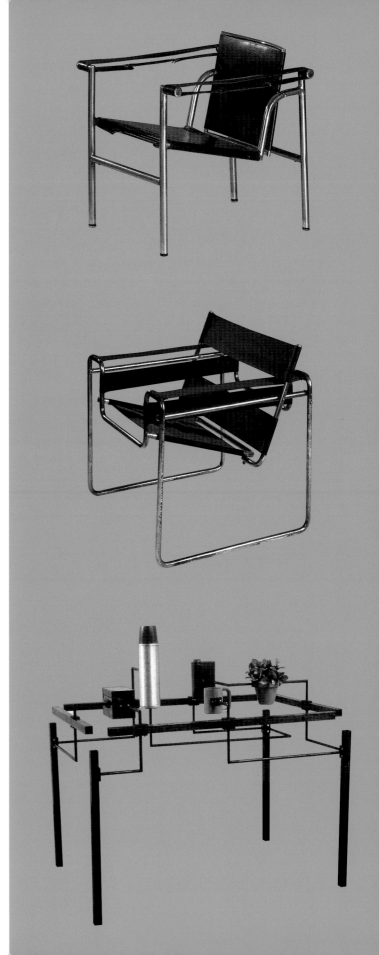

Although the Corbusier and Breuer chairs are some of the most recognizable artifacts of the first half of the twentieth century, perhaps the most iconic modern example is Mies's Barcelona Chair (see fig. 2.2). And if Tuttle was going to take aim at the other two, why not throw his hat into the ring with Mies as well? Tuttle's "Z" Chair of 1964 (fig. 2.18) was the perfect response—an object as elegantly reductive and breathtakingly engineered as it was mischievous. Where Mies played the cool, reserved Greek, interested in classical proportions and gracious enthronement, Tuttle showed himself to be the swashbuckling thrill seeker. Viewing both chairs in profile, Mies marks the spot with a balanced "X" while Tuttle favors the reckless "Z" of Zorro. The chairs beg for comparison, as each is made by the difficult joinery of welded, chromed steel with a leather sling seat and draws inspiration from mundane leaf springs found on trucks or tractors. Tuttle's chair, however, thrusts its Miesian predecessor into the present by introducing a dramatic cantilever and stripping the padded upholstery down to the bare minimum (banishing the buttoned-and-tufted look forever). The distinctive design of the "Z" Chair also provided arm support, in contrast to the armless Barcelona Chair, and has proven a fecund shape, spawning a panoply of variations over the years.

One of the most recent is the "Z" Chair of 1995 (fig. 2.19) which trades chrome for stainless steel and leather for rich pearwood. Gone is the one-piece seat/back sling in favor of a two-part support, and the exciting tension found in the cantilever of the earlier chair is ratcheted up considerably in the newer version. Here, rather than slouching toward one another, the steel parts bulge and expand as if ready to bounce off the floor. Adding to the agitated feel of the design are the threaded metal screws that pierce the floor-bound steel legs, lifting the chair off the ground like high-heeled shoes. These rubber-tipped modifiers "corrupt" the clean lines of the earlier chair, demonstrating that Tuttle was willing to "ruffle the feathers" of his own work as well as that of others. They make the design more contemporary, imbuing it with the sex appeal of a stiletto pump and accentuating the lines of the chair in much the same way that high heels alter a woman's posture. The screws contrast so drastically with the flow of the chair, however, that they also activate it as a sculpture once again, functioning in much the same way as the metal-tipped legs of Tuttle's early armchair (see fig. 2.5) and inviting the viewer to more closely examine what a chair can be.

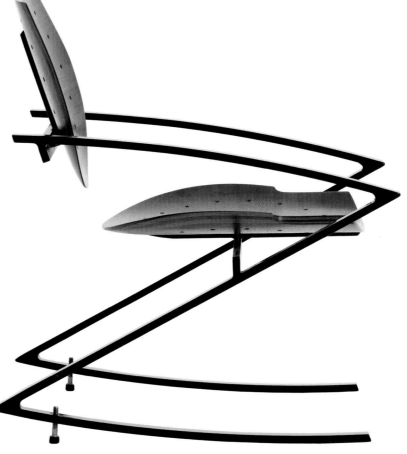

2.18 "Z" Chair (Prototype), 1964
Chrome-plated steel, leather
Produced by Carson-Johnson, Inc.,
Los Angeles, California
Collection of Joan and Jim Tanner

2.19 "Z" Chair, 1995
Stainless steel, pearwood
Produced by Bud Tullis, Solvang,
California, and Tri-County Fabrication,
Santa Barbara, California
This chair no longer exists

2.20 Nonna Rocking Chair, 1972
Bent beech, chrome-plated tubular steel, cowhide
Produced by Strässle International, Switzerland
Collection of Joanne and Brian Rapp

The Nonna Rocking Chair (1972; fig. 2.20) was equally positioned against convention, directly aping the oft-copied Thonet bentwood rocking chair originally designed in the 1880s (fig. 2.21) with a contemporary upgrade to tubular chrome. In his version, Tuttle transfers all the rocking surface to the tubular metal, while the bentwood elements never touch the ground, only coming into contact with the body. From an ergonomic standpoint, this makes great sense, as the contact of warm wood with the skin is much preferred over cold steel, but symbolically, it signals a new technological era where machines do the real work. One of the ingenious aspects of this design is the way in which it visually captures the motion of a rocking chair, as the looping form of the metal is nearly echoed in the wood portion, although they are kept tantalizingly out of sync. When at rest, the chair seems to describe the range of motion it can achieve when activated. It is as close as a chair has come to a Cubist representation of motion, recalling Marcel Duchamp's *Nude Descending a Staircase* or the time-lapse photographs of Eadweard Muybridge.

Perhaps more than any other chair, however, the Laminata of 1977 (fig. 2.22) expresses a core impulse in Tuttle's oeuvre to grapple with history and wrestle it into the present on his own terms. In this masterful design, he aggressively and almost violently recombines elements of classic modernist design in order to create an entirely new vision of an armchair. The Laminata is strongly defined by its perfectly proportioned, laminated wood armrests which are pulled into graceful curves that bend back under the seat to make a sturdy base. Formally, the contours of this fluid arm-to-leg composition recall the pristine cantilever

2.21 Designer unknown
Rocking Chair, Model No. 1, c. 1866
Beech, cane, leather
Produced by Gebruder Thonet, Vienna
Vitra Design Museum, Weil am Rhein

2.22 Laminata Chair, 1977
Bent laminated beech, tubular steel, leather
Produced by Strässle International, Switzerland
Collection of Julia Emerson

of Mies van der Rohe's MR 20 Armchair (1927; fig. 2.23), while there is a definite material connection to Alvar Aalto's Armchair 400 (1935–1936; fig. 2.24), which also features laminated wood arms in a similar configuration. The earlier chairs have a purity of character that comes from their consciously limited palette of materials—for Mies, chrome and leather (or cane); for Aalto, wood and upholstery—but Tuttle brazenly mixes the warmth of wood with the chill of chrome so that the wood elements are pierced through by the unrelenting strength of metal. This forced marriage of opposites is further emphasized by the way that the laminated wood curve is held in tension by the penetrating chrome chassis, locked into place at the sites of contact with large round washers. This seems to tempt viewers to read it as a Frankenstein-like repair job, cobbled together with whatever was lying around, but the end product is anything but haphazard. The juxtaposition of parts and forms is bracingly dynamic, and the more one studies it, the curves and angles, natural and man-made surfaces, tension and repose cohere to suggest a new standard of beauty, one containing a decided element of danger. Tuttle had girded sensual woods with rational metals in earlier designs, and this tendency belies a certain sexy, even kinky, treatment of his materials. As with the perverse desire to linger over car accidents portrayed in J.G. Ballard's contemporaneous novel *Crash* (1973), and David Cronenberg's later film of the same name, or the similar aesthetic explored from time to time by Helmut Newton in his photography (fig. 2.25), there is an adrenaline rush that accompanies the appreciation of Tuttle's beautiful collisions.

2.23 Ludwig **Mies van der Rohe** (1886–1969)
MR 20 Armchair, 1927
Chrome-plated tubular steel, leather
Produced by Berliner Metallgewerbe
Josef Müller, Berlin
The Museum of Modern Art, New York;
Gift of Edgar Kaufmann, Jr. (20.1949)

2.24 Alvar **Aalto** (1898–1976)
Armchair 400, 1935–1936
Bent laminated birch, sprung
and upholstered seat and back
Produced by Artek, Helsinki

2.25 Helmet **Newton** (b. 1920)
Photograph from *Vogue*
(February 1995)

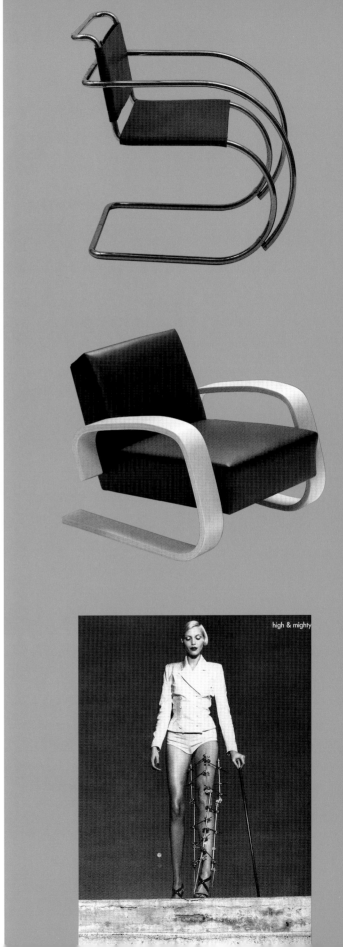

2.26 Tractor Seat Jazz, 1977
Painted tractor seat, painted tubular steel
Produced by A. Schonenberger, Switzerland
Collection of Merrily Peebles and Paul Roberts

Tractor Seat Jazz (fig. 2.26) also from 1977 puts forth an even more dangerous vision of discord, making the Laminata look positively composed and balanced by comparison. Here Tuttle does seem to be actively courting an image of dissonance and chaos, as disparate sections of tubular metal momentarily cohere in a chair-like structure. The ready-made tractor seat and faux-messy paint job similarly conspire to conjure a weekend garage project gone awry, but in the end, the ingenious integration of form and function leaves no doubt that this is an acutely considered artistic statement, albeit one with a wonderful spirit of spontaneity. Tuttle's use of the tractor seat calls to mind the dadaistic combinations of off-the-shelf materials that the Castiglioni brothers brought to their furniture design in the 1950s and 1960s (fig. 2.27), but the freewheeling exuberance of Tuttle's chair makes the otherwise witty Castiglionis look like arch academics. The designer revisited the folly ten years later in Jazz II Ph.D. (1987; see fig. 1.59), substituting for the tractor seat a gridded one that seems derived from racket sports. In this version, the tubular metal swoops and curves with the same lack of inhibition seen in the former but has a more additive, collaged quality. A spray of thin metal rods connect the legs near floor level, while higher up a metal ring is added to terminate an upward thrust of the structure. Other rings keep the seat material in place, and a yellow cotter pin keeps the back support from coming apart at the seams. It is a chair masquerading as a whimsical sculptural statement, assuring visual stimulation and providing gravitational relief for the body in one fell swoop.

2.27 Achille (b. 1918)
and Pier Giacomo (1913–1968)
Castiglioni
Mezzadro [sharecropper] Stool, 1954–1957
Chrome-plated steel, beech, painted steel
Produced by Zanotta s.p.a., Nova Milanese
Vitra Design Museum, Weil am Rhein

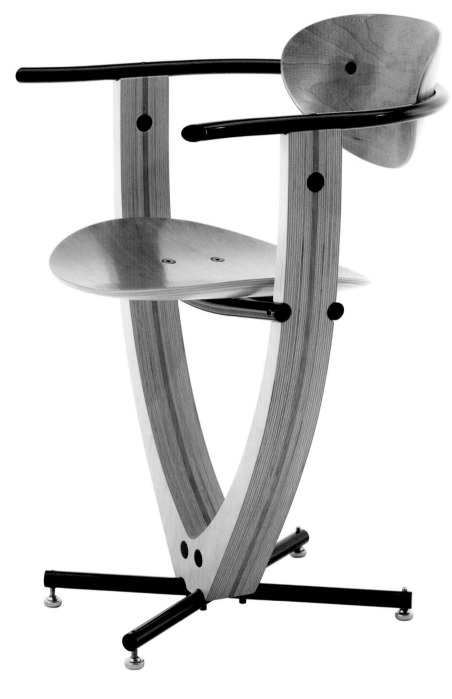

2.28 "66/85" Dining Chair, 1985
Cherry, cane, painted steel
Produced by Bud Tullis, Solvang, California
Collection of Robert and Ann Diener

2.29 "V" Dining Chair, 1998
Appleply, cherry, painted steel
Produced by Bud Tullis, Solvang,
California, and Tri-County Fabrication,
Santa Barbara, California
Collection of Edmund Austin DePree

Tuttle frequently revisited earlier designs, especially those he found to offer promise of improvement or reinterpretation. The various reincarnations of the "Z" Chair have already been discussed, and over the years there have been numerous iterations of the groundbreaking "66" Chair, first introduced in 1966. Tuttle's "66/85" Dining Chair (1985; fig. 2.28), for instance, is one of his most radical designs and an excellent example of the designer's interest in pushing comfortable, acceptable forms into new territory. Like some of the aforementioned works, it alludes to historical sources, in this case the economical connection of arms and back found in the Round Chair of 1949 by important Danish designer Hans Wegner (fig. 2.30). This chair, epitomizing the good clean looks of Scandinavian design, was widely sold and copied and could therefore be seen as ripe for a Tuttle intervention. Tuttle was as obsessed with beautiful craftsmanship and construction as his Nordic peers, and his chair does not lack in detailing. In some variations of his chair, Wegner used decorative joinery in the middle of the back piece, a feature Tuttle also includes, but the Tuttle chair takes a more aggressive posture with its pointed (almost dangerous) arms, abruptly contoured transition from back to arm, and the precarious stance of its clothespin legs. The most potent element of the chair, however, and one that characterizes some of Tuttle's most powerful later works, is the inclusion of a sturdy metal brace under the seat. This element, with its cold, shiny surface and considerable proportions, is another prosthetic device, shifting the image of the wood chair toward a futuristic cyborg seating tool that only nominally needs to feature wood. Although gracefully shaped and impeccably connected to the other parts of the chair, this steel piece reads as a foreign interloper portending all manner of changes to the existing order.

2.30 Hans J. **Wegner** (b. 1914)
Round Chair, 1949
Beech and cane
Produced by Johannes Hansen, Denmark
Philadelphia Museum of Art:
Gift of Carl L. Steele, acc. no. 1972-5-2

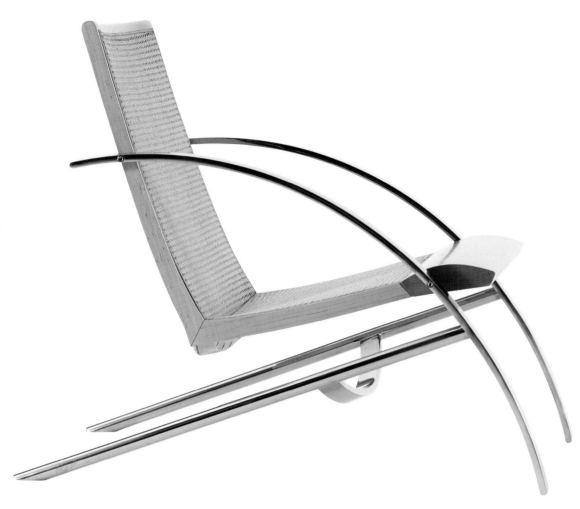

One of the latest versions of the "66" Chair is the "V" Dining Chair (1998; fig. 2.29). It echoes its predecessor in its positioning of arm and back pieces on top of a tenuous fulcrum, but in the newer model, the double clothespin pieces that made up the leg structure of the "66/85" are subsumed into a single wishbone of hefty laminated plywood that dips under the seat rather than flanking it. The legs are excised completely, supplanted with a simple X-base that hugs the floor. The genealogy is evident, but as is always the case with Tuttle, older designs are never brought back for nostalgia's sake, only if they can offer new insights for a new period. The designer's successful Arco Chair, first introduced by the Swiss furniture company Strässle in 1976, has also been reworked over the years, sometimes with only slight interventions to do with the materials, such as the Arco II from 1997 (fig. 2.31). This chair, perhaps unsurprisingly, in its use of a slender wood-framed seat suspended within the elegant arcs of highly polished steel, carries the DNA of Tuttle's very early Dining Chair of 1959 (see fig. 2.7) whose beautifully articulated seat and elongated proportions are reinterpreted in the later lounger. The Arco II's seat and back have been even more recently revived in the Low Chair of 1998 (fig. 2.32), albeit with slight modifications to the caning. As further evidence of the designer's revisionist bent, the Low Chair also recalls the iconic Nonna Rocking Chair in its lively suggestion of fluid motion. Yet another recent revisitation of the Nonna can be found in the rhythmic curves of Tuttle's 1997 Rocking Chair.

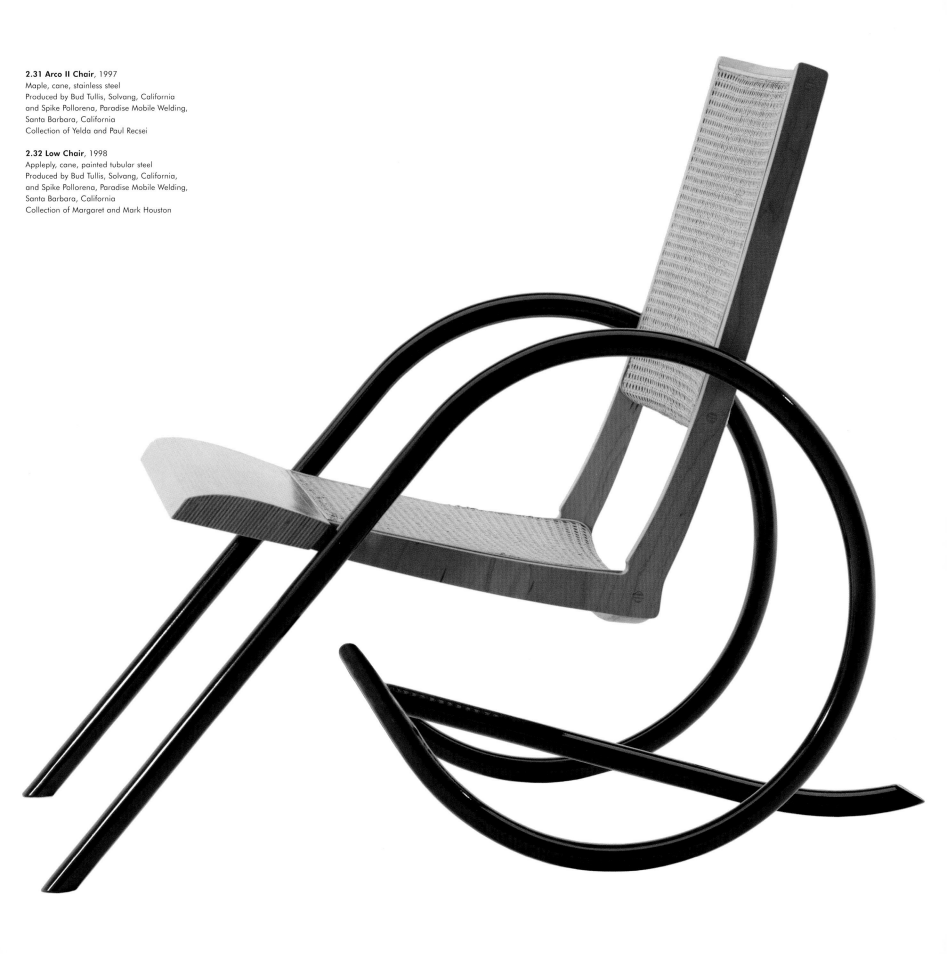

2.31 Arco II Chair, 1997
Maple, cane, stainless steel
Produced by Bud Tullis, Solvang, California
and Spike Pollorena, Paradise Mobile Welding,
Santa Barbara, California
Collection of Yelda and Paul Recsei

2.32 Low Chair, 1998
Appleply, cane, painted tubular steel
Produced by Bud Tullis, Solvang, California,
and Spike Pollorena, Paradise Mobile Welding,
Santa Barbara, California
Collection of Margaret and Mark Houston

2.33 Chaise Longue, 1995
Cherry, tubular steel, upholstery
Produced by Bud Tullis, Solvang, California
Collection of Julia Emerson

2.34 Chaise Longue, 1996
Maple, cane, tubular steel, upholstery
Produced by Bud Tullis, Solvang, California
Collection of the Andina Family

2.35 Spring Chair, 1991
Laminated birch ply, painted steel,
ultrasuede upholstery
Produced by Bud Tullis, Solvang, California
Collection of Carol L. Valentine

Indeed, the 1990s saw the designer at play with many motifs culled from his past repertoire, matched with a heightened sense of formal experimentation. For example, a second classic from Tuttle's work with the Strässle company, the Anaconda of 1970 (see fig. 1.47), with its marvelously spare streamlining of legs, arms, and back and visually precarious single back leg, gave rise to two emblematic works from the 1990s. The Chaise Longue of 1995 (fig. 2.33)—followed by a mirror image in 1996 (fig. 2.34)—and the Spring Chair of 1991 (fig. 2.35) derive from the structural logic of the Anaconda but take it to completely different ends. Both chairs substitute thick wooden dowels for the comparatively more slender chromed tubing of the Anaconda, and each makes mannered use of the leg-arm-back synthesis. The Chaise stretches the Anaconda into a luxurious recliner and cleverly transfers the junction of the arm pieces to floor level in a funny sublimation of the Anaconda's distinctive single back leg. The proportions have also changed dramatically from a utilitarian-minded lightness to a much more decadent expression of material. This difference has much to do with the intended use of the chairs—the Anaconda being a mobile dining chair and the Chaise a stationary lounger— but also appropriately reflects the decades in which they were made. As a lounge chair, the Spring Chair is also a much different object in its function than the Anaconda, but its genesis is similarly rooted in the earlier design. Like the Chaise Longue, it incorporates a loop of round-sectioned wood in exaggerated proportions, but its other constituent parts are placed in even stronger relief. Here,

angular black metal serves to counteract the organic embrace of the wood, playing hard and cool against soft and warm as in so many Tuttle designs. The single back leg of the Anaconda is again invoked, but its structural stability is even more daringly tested in the latter model, where a dangling tail of strap metal barely kisses the floor. As with so many of his other designs, Tuttle plays the voluptuous and conventionally beautiful against more discordant notes derived from industry to both activate the chair as a visually stimulating object and to propose new standards of aesthetic pleasure.

Looking back over his long and productive career, it becomes apparent that a dialogic agenda has been at work in Tuttle's furniture from the very start. His unwavering quest to design chairs and other objects that possessed the intellectual stimulation of sculpture and the familiar comforts required of useful things led him in innumerable directions and to a shocking number of successful solutions. It was his innate sense of artistic ambition that kept him from becoming complacent or falling back on conventions, and sometimes it was the challenge laid down by earlier pioneers of design that spurred him on to find new expressions capable of speaking to his time and place. For those that have had the opportunity to live with Tuttle furniture, such eloquence has enriched daily experience, and with the greater exposure offered by publications such as this, surely many more will feel privileged to listen in on the conversation.

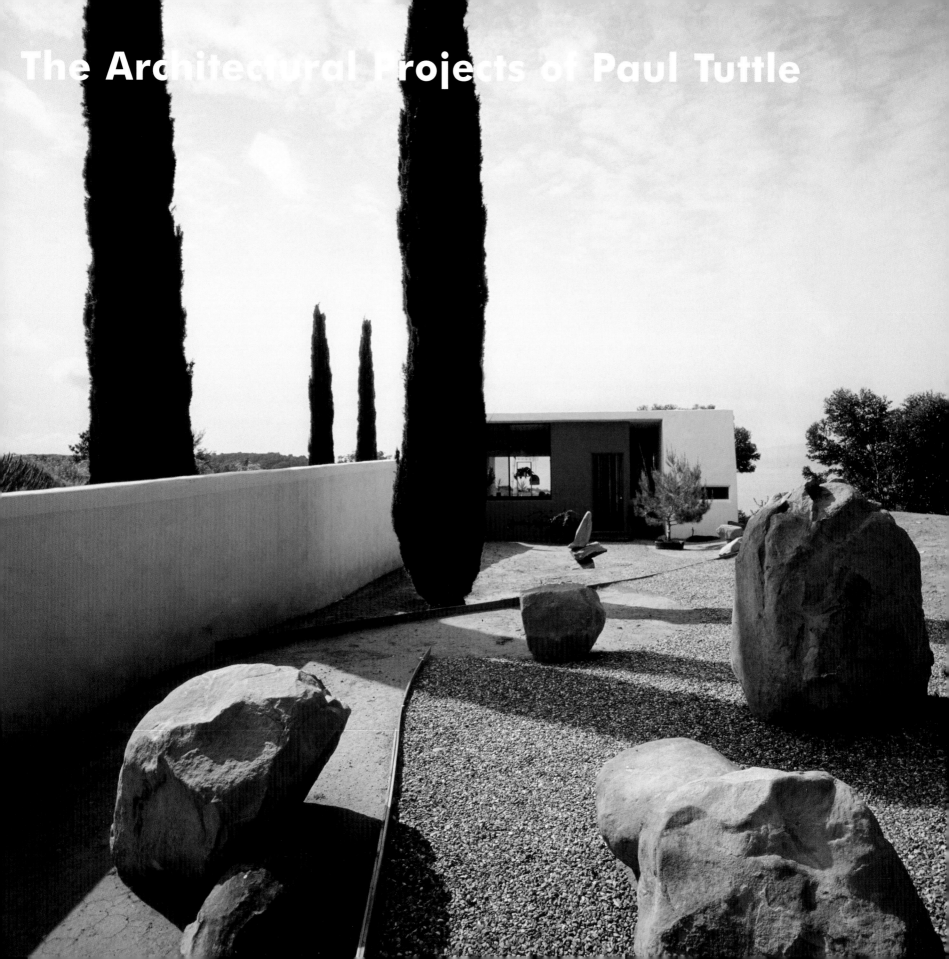

The Architectural Projects of Paul Tuttle

KURT G. F. HELFRICH

During the last seventy-five years there has been evolving a concept of building which has placed human needs, structural honesty, and a new understanding of space before any stylistic considerations.... We in California, especially the younger designers, have the great opportunity to inherit this treasure of beliefs, ideas, and discoveries and to carry further their logical developments.... If we are going to develop an architecture worthy of the terrain and the potential living pattern, we must be stern in our self-criticism and ask ourselves many questions. Alvin Lustig, 1947[1]

Paul Tuttle's executed architectural projects consist of a series of five residences constructed between 1959 and 1967 and a more recent collaboration completed in 1998—all of these nestled in the foothills and beaches surrounding Santa Barbara. Tuttle's houses are highly unique statements that, like his furniture designs, defy easy categorization. Powerfully melded to and shaped by their particular sites, his Santa Barbara houses are at once tectonic and sculptural. As the architectural historian David Gebhard has succinctly noted, they are "enlarge- ment[s]... of his finely-detailed pieces of furniture."[2] Tuttle himself commented on the fundamental unity between his architecture and furniture designs in the mid-1960s, remarking, "Often, my need to do a house...or a new piece of furniture is a way to extend a shape I have worked out in clay.... but it always leads me back to furniture, because I always design some for each house."[3] Gebhard included Tuttle's own studio/residence in his pioneering 1965 survey of architecture, *A Guide to Architecture in Southern California*, and eventually featured three of Tuttle's houses in his expanded 1977 guidebook to the region.[4]

Within the context of Southern California design, Gebhard saw Tuttle's houses as classic essays in "International Style" modernism that built upon the spare, elegant post-and-beam residences of Los Angeles designers associated with John Entenza's Case Study House program of the 1940s and 1950s.[5] At the same time, he noted that Tuttle's own 1962 studio/residence constituted a departure from such rigid stylistic categorization, viewing its sculptural, organic form as tied more closely to Mediterranean vernacular building traditions evoked by Santa Barbara's similar landscape and climate.[6]

While Paul Tuttle's architectural work has not been accorded the same scrutiny that his furniture has, it is nonetheless an important extension of his design career and was driven by his creative desire to explore the full impact that design has in our daily lives. His architectural work owes a debt to three mentors whose varied careers exposed him to the full potential that architecture could play in this process: graphic designer Alvin Lustig and architects Welton Becket and Thornton Ladd. Neglected today, they were major figures in Southern California's post–World War II develop- ment of a vital contemporary design ethos—part of the magic that Lustig would characterize as "California Modern."[7] Tuttle's architectural designs draw on and extend this "tradition," which was in essence a freedom from tradition, as embodied in the work of these three Southern California designers.

3.1 Exterior, c. 1977, Paul Tuttle studio/residence, Carpinteria, 1961–1962
Paul Tuttle, designer, with Robert Garland Jr., architect

3.2 Alvin Lustig in his Beverly Hills office, c. 1947

3.3 Alvin Lustig New Directions book jacket design for *Nightwood* (1946) by Djuna Barnes

As Marla Berns has noted in chapter 1 of this volume, Paul Tuttle's youthful interest in design began with a fascination with architecture and its tectonic potential—particularly the crisp structural forms of Robert Maillart's pre–World War II bridges in Switzerland.[8] Maillart's bridges were powerful examples of functional engineered sculpture—uniting two seemingly disparate fields in ways that Tuttle would later explore in his own furniture and residences. Following active service in India during World War II, Tuttle moved to Los Angeles in 1946 where he began attending classes—through the GI Bill—at the progressive Art Center School, then located on Seventh Street in downtown Los Angeles. During his short time there, Tuttle attended an advanced class taught by graphic and architectural designer Alvin Lustig (1915–1955). Although his career was cut short by his death at the early age of forty, Lustig was nonetheless hailed by contemporary critics, including Philip Johnson, as a unique and sensitive designer who defied easy categorization (fig. 3.2). His design work ranged from typography, including book cover and advertising layouts, to office and commercial interiors and buildings.[9]

Born in Denver, Lustig was raised in Los Angeles where he studied briefly at the Art Center School with Kem Weber in the early 1930s and with Frank Lloyd Wright in 1935 before traveling to New York where he freelanced as a graphic designer and worked as visual research director for *Look* magazine. Returning to the West Coast in 1946, Lustig opened a design office in Beverly Hills where he continued his graphic design work—including a number of innovative covers for the New Classic Series published by New Directions Books (fig. 3.3)—and collaborated on a number of architectural projects including commercial interiors and the Beverly-Landau Apartments, completed in 1949 with architect Sam Reisbord (fig. 3.4).[10]

In Los Angeles, Lustig became a highly influential teacher, first at the Art Center School and later at the University of Southern California. Opposed to what he saw as the tendency toward specialization within design education, he advocated a Bauhaus-inspired synthetic approach that emphasized what he termed "pure design" and incorporated techniques from the visual arts (particularly painting), as well as the manual arts. For Lustig, the greatest contemporary examples of pure design included the various chairs that Charles Eames created during the 1940s (fig. 3.5). Lustig felt that Eames's chairs were produced "with the greatest respect for material, the greatest respect for the technical process, the greatest respect for everything that he as a human being has been able to absorb about form and the meaning form-relationship provides."[11] As he taught his students, the most important challenge facing the modern designer was, in his opinion, to "remain free, as free as he possibly can, from the prejudices and ruts which affect so many others in the field of design. He must be constantly on guard, cleansing his mind of the tendency to relax into a routine format, ready to experiment, play, change and alter forms."[12] These were injunctions that found a strong resonance within Paul Tuttle's developing design approach.

While Tuttle spent only a brief period in Alvin Lustig's class at the Art Center School, Lustig subsequently hired him as a part-time employee in his Beverly Hills office. According to Tuttle, Lustig was fascinated by the way his young protégé's design creativity worked—particularly Tuttle's use of meticulous three-dimensional models, instead of drawings—to help explain his ideas. In spite of Tuttle's poor drafting skills, Lustig strongly believed in the young designer's creative potential. Tuttle's copy of the book surveying Lustig's book jacket designs for New Directions was inscribed by Lustig, "To Paul, with highest expectations."[13] Lustig remained in Los Angeles until 1951 when he returned to New York City where he continued his graphic and architectural work and taught design at Yale University. Struggling with an illness that left him completely blind in 1954, Lustig continued designing through his apprentices until his death the following year.[14] As Berns argues in chapter 1 of this volume, Lustig's impact on Tuttle's design philosophy was significant and enduring. Tuttle absorbed Lustig's passionate search for a synthetic approach that refused to view design as a series of specialized fields, attempting instead to unify seemingly disparate disciplines, ranging from typography to architecture. Summing up Lustig's impact, Tuttle noted, "his emphasis was, a simple sentence to the effect that if you analyze a problem thoroughly enough you get truly to a space where there isn't anything you can't do. And that was my criterion from that point on."[15]

Spurred on by his own creative urge—as well as Alvin Lustig's design precepts—Tuttle sought to educate himself as an architectural designer beginning in late 1948 with a five-and-a-half-month fellowship at Frank Lloyd Wright's Taliesin in Scottsdale, Arizona.[16] There he achieved distinction in Wright's eyes by his "naïve explorations," which included a unique enhancement of the design of his utilitarian outdoor tent through a series of wooden struts.[17] He also developed a lifelong passion for the desert landscape and an outdoor way of life. Returning to Los Angeles in 1950, Tuttle designed showroom interiors for the

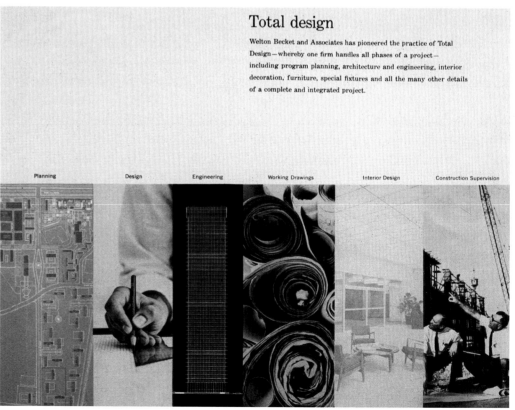

Total design

Welton Becket and Associates has pioneered the practice of Total Design—whereby one firm handles all phases of a project—including program planning, architecture and engineering, interior decoration, furniture, special fixtures and all the many other details of a complete and integrated project.

Planning   Design   Engineering   Working Drawings   Interior Design   Construction Supervision

Englishman, Arundel Clarke, followed by work for two Los Angeles architects, Welton Becket and Thornton Ladd, until his move to Santa Barbara in 1956. While working for these Los Angeles architects, Tuttle concentrated on designing interiors that helped solidify his uniquely intuitive approach—one that seamlessly knit furniture with building, structure, and landscape.

Tuttle's work for Welton Becket involved interior designs for branch stores of the Joseph Magnin Company built in new shopping center complexes in the San Francisco area, including Stonestown, Hillsdale, and Stanford. Becket (1902–1969) was a University of Washington trained architect who opened a practice with his Seattle classmate, Walter Wurdeman, in Los Angeles in 1933. Specializing in large-scale commercial and institutional projects, Wurdeman and Becket (known as Welton Becket and Associates following Wurdeman's death in 1948) designed what is still considered one of the most important prototypes in the United States for the post–World War II suburban department store, the Bullock's Department Store in Pasadena, completed in 1947 (fig. 3.6). The store's severe horizontal exterior belied its rich and decorative interior design, which sought to express "the California love of outdoor living" through the use of plant forms in interior wall decorations, the indoor use of "outdoor" materials, the utilization of daylight within the store, the creation of informal outdoor lounges, and the establishment of outdoor as well as indoor luncheon and tea facilities.[18] As *Time Magazine* noted, Wurdeman and Becket's design pioneered the abolishing of fixed partitions and central stockrooms (each department had its own) and the installing of direct package delivery to customer's automobiles to create a country-club-like environment and a new trend in department store design.[19]

By 1954 when Paul Tuttle worked for the firm, Welton Becket and Associates had a staff of 140 specialists including architects, engineers, draftsmen, interior designers, cost control experts, and economists.[20] That year, the firm was constructing fourteen shopping centers, including a fifteen million-dollar development project for Stanford University, which turned a piece of unused campus land in Palo Alto into a shopping center with two department stores, a supermarket, a medical building, and parking spaces for 5,500 automobiles. As a designer in Becket's firm, Paul Tuttle helped to pioneer the concept of "Total Design" on a corporate scale, participating in extensive background research by the office for the Joseph Magnin stores to determine the best "flow patterns" for the customers, the clerks, and the merchandise (fig. 3.7). For the Magnin stores, the firm designed not only the buildings but also their details including "display cases, counters, tie racks, door handles, the wallpaper, and even the plates in the buffet."[21] Tuttle worked on designs for these innovative store interiors including chairs, stools, and tables (see. fig. 1.17), as well as fixture and display cases, often arriving at work early to look over drawings produced by other departments.[22]

Tuttle's designs for Welton Becket and Associates introduced him to the world of architecture at the corporate level during the 1950s. His work for Pasadena architect and landscape designer Thornton Ladd (b. 1924), however, was more meaningful in the context of his own later work in the 1960s, as it was focused more on residential design including furniture, interior architectural details such as fireplaces, and outdoor sculpture. Tuttle's work for Ladd provided him with specific details and techniques that he would refine and expand in his Santa Barbara residences. Organized in 1954, Thornton Ladd & Associates, later known as **Ladd & Kelsey** (1959–1974), specialized in a wide array of building types, including residential, commercial, and institutional structures, as well as interior and landscape designs.[23]

Unlike Welton Becket and Associates, Thornton Ladd's office kept its architectural output at a small scale to ensure a craftsman level of design detail was maintained. The firm placed a great emphasis on its interior work, viewing interior design as "the sculpture of space into a three-dimensional continuum of living areas, each fashioned to fulfill its own function and still contribute and conform to the pattern of the whole."[24] Trained as an architect at the University of Southern California, Thornton Ladd had met Tuttle in Los Angeles in the early 1950s and greatly admired his design creativity. Later, he perceived Tuttle's contribution as integral to his firm's high-quality work. In the office profile, Ladd praised Tuttle's contribution to the firm's designs by noting "Custom-designed and built-in furniture—storage units, seating arrangements, even bathroom fixtures—are the final brush strokes with which the architect completes his canvas of integrated design."[25]

Thornton Ladd felt that the residence was the most complex and important design exercise that an architect faced: It is "the crucible in which truly creative innovations of contemporary architecture are originally evolved. In this sense the house is the architect's laboratory and as such represents one of the most dynamic and productive expressions of his talents."[26] Ladd's own hillside home (fig. 3.8) embodied these principles and commanded dramatic views of both downtown Los Angeles and Pasadena's Arroyo Seco. It was completed in 1952 and included a residence for his mother, Lillian, as well as a small rectangular steel-framed studio with sliding glass walls and canvas panels for himself.[27] While working for Ladd between 1955 and 1956, Tuttle lived in Ladd's studio (fig. 3.9) for which he designed

a number of furnishings that served as architectural elements to help reshape the interior spaces. Particularly noteworthy was the floating platform seating area for the studio's sitting room that Tuttle created (see fig. 1.14). While in Ladd's office, Tuttle also developed a special interest in the design of interior fireplaces. Tuttle's fireplaces were unique sculptural forms—made of beautifully finished materials—that served as distinctive features in Ladd's houses. Tuttle's interior designs for Ladd, including the fireplace in the Kurt Fring residence in Beverly Hills, were awarded a Progressive Architecture Residential Design award in 1956.[28]

Referred to as an "Etruscan monastery" by noted architectural critic and historian Sigfried Giedion, Ladd's "Hilltop" residence linked architecture and landscape through a rigorous exercise in geometry. Organized around the pure form of an open cube, it made use of horizontal and vertical planes, floating slabs and trellises, interlocking levels and terraces, squares and rectangles, walls and screens (figs. 3.10, 3.11).[29] In a statement about its overall organization, Ladd characterized the site plan as "a linked series of rectangles and squares, including a pool, a pavilion, gardens and a peristyle. No rules, no formulas, no styles were used; just a combining of those different parts in a way that best seemed to express the purpose they represent.... Through the intricate arrangement of levels, walls, grilles, and covered walks, the garden areas become individual outdoor 'rooms'—each with its own character but contributing to the [overall] architectural harmony."[30] As Ladd's office noted about the residence, "textured surfaces, integrated landscaping, and the illusion of levitation achieved by the use of 'floating' horizontal planes" helped fuse indoor and outdoor space into a single environmental complex.[31] These design elements and the overall philosophy would inform and suggest a number of important themes used in Tuttle's later residences in Santa Barbara.

3.8 "Hilltop," Thornton Ladd studio and residence, Pasadena, c. 1952
Thornton Ladd, architect
Collection of Thornton Ladd, Ojai

Paul Tuttle's independent architectural work began in 1959, after he had moved to Santa Barbara. His first commission was a spare and elegant pavilion design for a beach house in the nearby town of Carpinteria.[32] This and his other major architectural commissions—the design of four residences in the Santa Barbara region—were completed in the 1960s with the help of licensed local architects who created the working drawings and coordinated construction under Tuttle's careful, daily supervision. Tuttle's houses use planning features such as platform decks, sunken gardens, and interior courtyards, as well as unique pier structural systems, to create residences that are at once tectonic and sculptural—much like his furniture. In a 1997 interview about his architectural work, Tuttle noted, "I can't separate architecture, whether it's the detail or the structural systems...from the furniture, or the landscaping, or the way of life...I mean, they all come together as a family.

And I never, at any time, with any client...created a design where I didn't solve all these problems, simultaneously."[33]

Tuttle abandoned his architectural work during the late 1960s citing continued cost overruns and the difficulty of finishing structures to his exacting standards as the major factors.[34] Beginning in the early 1990s, following a hiatus of over twenty years, Paul Tuttle participated in a series of new projects in the Santa Barbara region that focused on the landscape and included design of outdoor hardscape elements including gates and staircases. Working with the Carpinteria architect Andy Neumann, Tuttle's last architectural project was the 1996–1998 renovation of the residence of Michele Andina in Montecito. In these endeavors, he retained the same focus on architecture as sculpture, expanding many of the design concepts first developed in his work of the 1960s.

3.9 Exterior view of studio entrance, 1956
"Hilltop" Thornton Ladd studio
and residence, Pasadena, 1950
Thornton Ladd, architect

3.10 View of swimming pool, 1956
"Hilltop" Thornton Ladd studio
and residence, Pasadena, 1952
Thornton Ladd, architect

3.11 View of interior courtyard, 1956
"Hilltop" Thornton Ladd studio
and residence, Pasadena, 1952
Thornton Ladd, architect

3.12 Exterior view of entrance facade, c. 1974,
George and Mary Lou Dangerfield beach house, Carpinteria, 1959
Paul Tuttle, designer, with Lawrence E. Harlow, architect

3.13 Elevations and sections, George and Mary Lou
Dangerfield beach house, Carpinteria, 1959
Paul Tuttle, designer, with Lawrence E. Harlow, architect
Drawing by Lawrence E. Harlow
Collection of George Gostavich, Carpinteria

3.14 Interior view of living room with fireplace,
George and Mary Lou Dangerfield beach house, Carpinteria, 1959
Paul Tuttle, designer, with Lawrence E. Harlow, architect

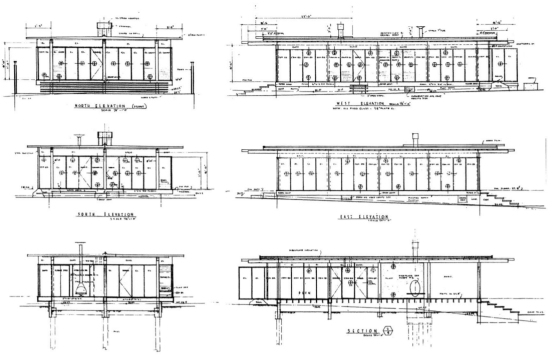

NORTH ELEVATION (FRONT)
SCALE 1/8" = 1'-0"

WEST ELEVATION SCALE 1/8" = 1'-0"
NOTE: ALL FIXED GLASS - 1/4" PLATE GL.

SOUTH ELEVATION
SCALE 1/8" = 1'-0"

EAST ELEVATION
SCALE 1/8" = 1'-0"

SECTION 1

Paul Tuttle's first independent architectural commission—done in collaboration with the architect Lawrence E. Harlow, a former associate in Thornton Ladd's office—was for a pavilion-like beach house nestled among oversized boulders in Carpinteria (fig. 3.12). Completed in 1959, it was built as a writing studio for Pulitzer Prize-winning historian George Dangerfield—a faculty member at the University of California, Santa Barbara—and his wife, Mary Lou. In the Dangerfield beach house, Tuttle developed an innovative pier structural system of cantilevered vertical wooden posts anchored to the foundation that served as an aesthetic device in its own right (fig. 3.13). The deceptively lightweight appearance of this pier system—enhanced by the use of glass clerestory windows—allowed the structure's roof to seemingly float or hover on its site. The beach house also draws on the spare orthogonal geometry characteristic of Ladd's earlier residence and studio.

Inside the house, Tuttle designed all of the furniture including two specially constructed built-in bunk beds matching the interior color scheme consisting of dark stained wooden posts, red crossbeams in the ceiling, and natural cork flooring. He also created a freestanding, poured-concrete, cylindrical fireplace—originally painted white—with oval openings on two sides serving as a signature curved sculptural element as well as a functional divider (fig. 3.14) that helped to break the main space into living and dining areas. Commenting on the unity of the house's design and furnishings, *Los Angeles Times* art critic Henry J. Seldis noted, "Everywhere in the structure Tuttle has concerned himself with the visual satisfaction of the owners along with the specific use to which each room will be put. A table, desk or chair is as much a part of the total design as the beach front or street approach."[35]

3.15 Exterior view, George and Mary Lou Dangerfield
residence, Carpinteria, 1960
Paul Tuttle, designer, with Serifo John Menegon, architect

DANGERFIELD RESIDENCE, CARPINTERIA, 1960

In 1960 Tuttle—in association with the architect Serifo John Menegon—completed a residence for George and Mary Lou Dangerfield and their growing family. The cube-like pavilion with a central open court (fig. 3.15), which eliminated the need for internal hallways, was set on a simple stucco-covered base perched on the edge of a hill overlooking the ocean.

PAUL TUTTLE STUDIO/RESIDENCE, CARPINTERIA, 1961–1962

Nestled in a cleft in the rolling foothills above Carpinteria, Tuttle's own retreat, completed in 1962 with the Santa Barbara architect Robert Garland Jr., was constructed adjacent to the Dangerfield residence. The studio/residence (fig. 3.1) was designed as a sloping, one-room box, the 550-square-foot structure includes a dining/work area, a living area, a Pullman kitchen, bathroom, and rear terrace. To reinforce the sculptural nature of the design, Tuttle originally intended to construct the house as a shell of lightweight sprayed concrete, but costs forced him to use a more conventional stud frame construction, the walls and roof of which were covered with plaster. Inside, the white walls, the wooden beams, the polished concrete floor covered by sheepskin rugs, the spare furnishings—including platforms serving as sitting and sleeping areas—were all carefully selected by Tuttle to create a unified design vision (fig. 3.17). Tuttle included a long horizontal band of glass—which he termed a solar window—set at a low height along the studio's western wall to allow light into the space as well as views of the surrounding landscape. Outside, he planted tall cypress trees to serve as foils to the horizontality of the structure. He also selected boulders, which he later painted, to create a carefully landscaped processional space leading to the studio's entrance.

In 1965 a critic characterized the residence as "a study in leanness and ruthless selectivity...as distinctly the owner's own as his fingerprints."[36] The long exterior white wall (fig. 3.16) at once anchors the structure to its hillside setting and extends the presence of the small box into the surrounding landscape—as one critic has poetically noted, "holding firm against the forces of land air and sea."[37] The exterior wall is, in turn, playfully broken by the curved notched opening where it joins the house to provide Tuttle with a view of the mountains from his interior desk. The rear terrace off Tuttle's sleeping area affords spectacular ocean views. Rarely satisfied with his own creative efforts, Tuttle was pleased by the design of his studio/residence and often playfully referred to the way the structure integrated itself within its setting and his own personal needs as "this white oneness."[38]

3.16 Exterior showing wall, Paul Tuttle studio/
residence, Carpinteria, 1961–1962
Paul Tuttle designer, with Robert Garland Jr., architect

3.17 Interior with sleeping platform, c. 1977,
Paul Tuttle studio/residence, Carpinteria, 1961–1962
Paul Tuttle, designer, with Robert Garland Jr., architect

DOUWE STUURMAN AND PHYLLIS PLOUS RESIDENCE, CARPINTERIA, 1965

Tuttle's design for the Stuurman-Plous residence (figs. 3.18–3.20), completed in 1965 with the Santa Barbara architect Richard Bliss Nelson, is an enlarged version of his own one-room studio/residence. Here he carefully designed the house around its sloping natural site and deliberately placed it over portions of Toro Creek to further enhance its oneness with the surrounding landscape. As in his own residence, Tuttle made use of a long exterior wall—this time with an arched doorway—to tie the main house and the bedroom wing to its sloping site (fig. 3.19).

The one-story, L-shaped structure is cleverly organized around a sunken interior court making use of floating platforms at different levels (fig. 3.18) to knit the spaces together. Plantings from the creek bed—including trees—grow up between the platforms, breaking down the traditional barriers between landscape and building.

3.18 (Opposite) Exterior walkway, c. 1974, Douwe Stuurman and Phyllis Plous residence, Carpinteria, 1965
Paul Tuttle, designer, with Richard Bliss Nelson, architect

3.19 (Top) Exterior wall, c. 1974, Douwe Stuurman and Phyllis Plous residence, Carpinteria, 1965
Paul Tuttle, designer, with Richard Bliss Nelson, architect

3.20 (Bottom) Exterior detail of wall with doorway, c. 1974, Douwe Stuurman and Phyllis Plous residence, Carpinteria, 1965
Paul Tuttle, designer, with Richard Bliss Nelson, architect

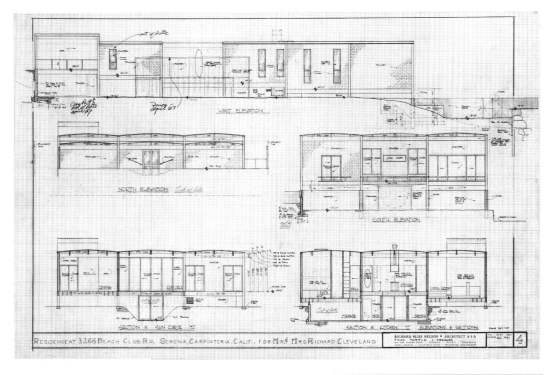

Tuttle's last built project during the 1960s, a beach house for the marine photographer Dick Cleveland and his wife, Tukey, was completed in 1967 with architect Richard Bliss Nelson (fig. 3.23). As previously noted, for this house, as with all of his architectural designs, Tuttle collaborated with a local licensed architect. He would develop the overall program by providing scaled drawings including plans, elevations, and key details. The associated architect would then create the final working drawings (fig. 3.22) and construct the house with Tuttle's meticulous oversight, including daily visits to the construction site.[39] Nelson's drawings show Tuttle's scheme for the rectangular H-shaped house whose wooden shingle-clad exterior and arched roof (set atop open wood trusses extending the length of the house) was built on a system of wood pilings specifically designed for a narrow sloping site overlooking the ocean. Entering via a bridge leading from a carport at street level to the house below, one progressed through a front door with abstract geometric patterning and then through a series of interior courts (fig. 3.21) and rooms at different levels to reach the swimming pool with its spectacular view to the ocean beyond. Tuttle's unique combination of window and beam details in these interior courts is typical of his skill in blending structure with pattern to create an abstracted flat relief that becomes sculptural (fig. 3.24).

3.21 (Opposite) View of interior court, Richard C. Cleveland beach house, Carpinteria, 1966–1967
Paul Tuttle, designer, with Richard Bliss Nelson, architect

3.22 (Top) Elevations and sections, Richard C. Cleveland beach house, Carpinteria, 1966–1967
Paul Tuttle, designer, with Richard Bliss Nelson, architect
Pencil and colored pencil on paper
Collection of Richard Bliss Nelson, Palm Desert, California

3.23 (Above) Exterior view of southern elevation showing pool, Richard C. Cleveland beach house, Carpinteria, 1966–1967
Paul Tuttle, designer, with Richard Bliss Nelson, architect
Collection of Richard Bliss Nelson, Palm Desert, California

3.24 (Right) Interior court window and beam detail, Richard C. Cleveland beach house, Carpinteria, 1966–1967
Paul Tuttle, designer, with Richard Bliss Nelson, architect

3.25 Exterior view of garage and entrance facade,
Michele Andina residence alteration, Montecito, 1996–1998
Paul Tuttle, designer, with Andy Neumann, architect

3.26a,b details of Interior view of staircase, Michele Andina
residence alteration, Montecito, 1996–1998
Paul Tuttle, designer, with Andy Neumann, architect

In the mid-1990s, Paul Tuttle, in collaboration with the Carpinteria-based architect Andy Neumann, renovated an existing single-story structure into a two-story guesthouse commanding spectacular ocean views from the Montecito foothills above Carpinteria (fig. 3.25). Asked originally to add only a second floor master bedroom, bath, and study, Tuttle expanded the program to include an airy open double-height second-story space capped by a vaulted roof (fig. 3.27) and a garage with an open outdoor deck above. As Neumann has recently noted, "The barrel vaulted ceiling evolved into a segmented 'barrel' that allows for tall north facing windows looking up to the dramatic mountains above. The curved ceiling is plastered white reminiscent of Greek architecture and has an abstract character with modernist roots with which Mikki Andina feels comfortable."[40] Recognizing the heightened importance of the rear (garage) entrance, Tuttle also designed a unique open interior staircase (fig. 3.26a,b), the sculptural form of which ingeniously incorporates a solid wooden log as its central support and cleverly maintains an unobstructed view from the new main entrance into the double-story barrel-vaulted space. As a part of the project, the driveway and surrounding landscaping were also renovated.

Paul Tuttle's six major executed architectural projects represent only a fraction of his total design output but are, nonetheless, a vital component in understanding the breadth of his artistic creativity and his fundamental belief in the power of design to improve all aspects of people's lives. Despite an innate reticence that often led him to downplay his architectural designs because of his lack of a formal architectural degree as well as his poor drafting skills, Tuttle's residences are compelling architectural statements

3.27 (Above) Interior second-floor vaulted
ceiling, Michele Andina residence alteration, Montecito, 1996–1998
Paul Tuttle, designer, with Andy Neumann, architect

3.28 (Opposite, top) Exterior view, Warren
and Katherine Tremaine house, Montecito, 1947–1948
Richard Joseph Neutra (1892–1970), architect

3.29 (Opposite, bottom) Exterior view of main house,
Barton Myers residence and studio, Montecito, 1996–1998
Barton Myers (b. 1934), architect

that continue to serve as benchmarks of creative contemporary design within the Santa Barbara region. Employing sculptural elements including interior floating platforms, specially designed fireplaces and staircases, as well as planning features such as sunken gardens and interior courtyards, his architectural designs helped blur traditional distinctions that still exist between furniture and structure, and indoor and outdoor spaces. Perhaps, then, it is this individualistic and sustained freedom from architectural convention that best captures the essence of Tuttle's design creativity—embodied in the excitement of what Alvin Lustig had termed "California Modern."

Firmly rooted in the landscape and topography of Santa Barbara, it is no accident that the bulk of Paul Tuttle's houses were created on or near the native oak and chaparral terrain of Toro Canyon Road. Toro Canyon was then a pristine and undeveloped part of Santa Barbara County. It served as home to a number of talented artists and intellectuals, and remained outside the jurisdiction of stylistic controls devised beginning in the 1960s for Santa Barbara's historic Pueblo Viejo district. Tuttle's six houses are important examples within the currently underexamined—but thriving—legacy of modern architecture in Santa Barbara. Viewed within the context of contemporary local residences that have achieved international recognition including Richard Neutra's Warren Tremaine House (1948; fig. 3.28), and the more recent Crawford House (1991) by Morphosis, and Myers Residence (1998) by Barton Myers Associates, Inc. (fig. 3.29), Paul Tuttle's six houses stand in their own right as unique and elegant contributions beautifully synthesizing traditional and contemporary elements in an understated manner that still resonates within our own age's continued search for a regionally meaningful and environmentally sensitive design.

NOTES

Unless otherwise noted, all interviews were conducted
by the author.

1 Alvin Lustig, "California Modern," in Holland R. Melson Jr.,
The Collected Writings of Alvin Lustig (New York: Thistle Press,
1958), 82–83. Lustig's essay was originally published in
Design (October 1947).

2 David Gebhard and Robert Winter, *A Guide to Architecture
in Southern California* (Los Angeles: The Los Angeles County
Museum of Art, 1965), L 3, 19, 20.

3 D.W., "Focus on Decoration: Paul Tuttle," *House Beautiful*
108 (October 1966): 223.

4 See David Gebhard and Robert Winter, *A Guide to
Architecture in Southern California,* L 3, 19, and pl. 78.
David Gebhard and Robert Winter, *A Guide to Architecture
in Los Angeles and Southern California* (Santa Barbara
and Salt Lake City: Peregrine Smith, Inc., 1977), 575. Four
of Tuttle's residences are featured in Bob Easton and Wayne
McCall, eds. *Santa Barbara Architecture: From Spanish
Colonial to Modern* (Santa Barbara: Capra Press, 1975),
212–214.

5 David Gebhard and Robert Winter, *A Guide to Architecture
in Los Angeles and Southern California,* 576.

6 Ibid., 575. Tuttle recalled that the organic form of the studio was inspired by vernacular buildings he had seen while
on a recent trip to Greece—particularly the white houses
found on the island of Mykonos. Interview with Paul Tuttle,
Santa Barbara, July 2001.

7 Alvin Lustig, "California Modern," 79–84.

8 Paul Tuttle first became aware of Maillart's designs through
publications while serving as a librarian for the US Army in
India during World War II.

9 On Alvin Lustig, see Holland R. Melson Jr., *The Collected
Writings of Alvin Lustig*; James Laughlin and Alvin Lustig,
*Book Jackets by Alvin Lustig for New Directions Books with
Statements by James Laughlin and Alvin Lustig* (New York:
Gotham Mart Press, 1947); and the exhibition catalog
by Peter Dodge, *Alvin Lustig: An Exhibition of His Work*
(Minneapolis: Walker Art Center, 1950).

10 For an interesting account of Lustig's philosophy and
return to Los Angeles, see "About the Career of a Young Man
with an Inquiring Mind: Alvin Lustig, Designer," *Interiors* 106
(September 1946): 68–75.

11 Alvin Lustig, "Designing, a Process of Teaching," in
Holland R. Melson Jr., *The Collected Writings of Alvin Lustig.*

12 Alvin Lustig, "What is a Designer?" *Type Talks* 76 (May
1954): 2–6. Lustig was adamant about the danger of over-
specialization in design education, as he noted in 1946,
"The words graphic designer, architect, or industrial designer
stick in my throat giving me a sense of limitation, of specialization within the specialty, of a relationship to society and
form itself that is unsatisfactory and incomplete. This inade-
quate set of terms to describe an active life reveals only par-
tially the still undefined nature of the designer." Alvin Lustig,
"Introductory Statement," in Holland R. Melson Jr., *The
Collected Writings of Alvin Lustig.* (This statement originally
appeared in *Interiors* [September 1946]).

13 See *Book jackets by Alvin Lustig for New Directions Books
with Statements by James Laughlin and Alvin Lustig.* Tuttle's
inscribed copy is in the Paul Tuttle Collection, Architecture and
Design Collection, University Art Museum, UCSB. I thank
Marla Berns for bringing this to my attention.

14 On Lustig's early death see, "Alvin Lustig, 40, Designer,
is Dead," *New York Times* (December 5, 1955) and his obitu-
ary in the *Architectural Forum* 104 (January 1956): 25.

15 Marla Berns, interview with Paul Tuttle, Santa Barbara,
October 1997.

16 Tuttle recalled having been introduced to Wright by
William Bernouli following a lecture Wright gave in Saint
Louis in the autumn of 1949. Interview with Paul Tuttle, Santa
Barbara, July 2001. Tuttle is listed as having been a member
of the Taliesin Fellowship from October? 1948 until May
1949. See the entry on Paul Tuttle in the privately printed
brochure by Elizabeth B. Kassler, *The Taliesin Fellowship:
A Directory of Members, 1932–1982* (Princeton, NJ: Privately
published, 1981) in the Paul Tuttle Collection, Architecture
and Design Collection, University Art Museum, UCSB.

17 Maeve Slavin, "Productive Design: Paul Tuttle Out in the
Open," *Interiors* (August 1980): 80.

18 "Bullock's Pasadena: A Fairyland for Shopper" *Southwest
Builder and Contractor* (September 26, 1947): 8–11, 22.

19 "Walt and Welt" *Time Magazine* 51 (March 1, 1948):
76–77.

20 "Busy Becket" *Newsweek* (March 9, 1953): 71

21 Ibid., 72. See also the firm's publication *Welton Becket
and Associates, Architects and Engineers* (n.d.) for a fuller
account of their concept of "Total Design," which they defined
to include "program planning, architecture and engineering,
interior decoration, furniture, special fixtures and all the many
other details of a complete and integrated project." Becket's
approach drew on organizational methods pioneered by the
firm of Skidmore, Owings & Merrill (SOM) established in
Chicago and New York in 1939, as well as the collaborative
design process espoused by Walter Gropius at Harvard during the 1940s and embodied in his firm, TAC (The Architects
Collaborative), established in Cambridge in 1946.

22 The Joseph Magnin store in Stonestown, California—which may have included interior designs and furnishings by Tuttle—was featured in a lavishly illustrated article appearing in *Architectural Record* in 1953, see "New Chapter in Stores Story: Joseph Magnin Store in Stonestown," *Architectural Record* 114 (December 1953): 144–53. Interview with Andy Neumann, Carpinteria, October 2002.

23 In 1974 the firm became Ladd, Kelsey, and Woodard. Thornton Ladd retired from active practice in 1981.

24 David Parry, ed.,*Thornton Ladd & Associates, Architects* (n.d.), 39.

25 Ibid., 46.

26 Ibid., 5

27 Ladd's studio was completed in 1950 according to Frank Harris and Weston Bonenberger, *A Guide to Contemporary Architecture in Southern California* (Los Angeles: Watling & Company, 1951), 21.

28 "P/A Design Survey for 1956 and Third Annual Design Awards Program," *Progressive Architecture* 37 (January 1956): 85.

29 "A Geometric House in the Romantic Tradition," *House and Home* 4 (December 1953):119.

30 Thornton Ladd quoted in "Progress Report: The Work of Ladd and Kelsey," *Progressive Architecture* (December 1959): 110.

31 *Thornton Ladd and Associates, Architects* (n.d.), 4.

32 Tuttle arrived in Santa Barbara in 1956 and was first listed in the Santa Barbara *City Directory* in 1957 as a designer with an office at 314 East Carillo Street. Following his move to Santa Barbara, Tuttle also worked briefly in the office of the architect Lutah Maria Riggs (1896–1984). Fellow employee, architect Richard Bliss Nelson recalls he stayed only a few months as Riggs was "looking for a draftsman and Paul Tuttle was beyond that." Interview with Richard Bliss Nelson, Rancho Mirage, August 2001.

33 Marla Berns, interview with Paul Tuttle, Santa Barbara, October 1997.

34 Paul Tuttle quoted in Maeve Slavin, "Productive Design: Paul Tuttle out in the Open," 83.

35 Henry J. Seldis, "Design: A Beach Pavilion By Paul Tuttle," *Art in America* (1961): 78–79. Photographs of the house were also featured in the exhibition sponsored by the Long Beach Museum of Art *Arts of Southern California*, held in March 1961.

36 Henry J. Seldis, "Young Man on a Mountain: Paul Tuttle, Furniture Designer," *House Beautiful* (July 1965): 62–63.

37 Dan MacMasters, "Mesa Magic by Paul Tuttle" *Los Angeles Times*, Home Section (January 15, 1978).

38 Ibid.

39 Interview with Richard Bliss Nelson, Rancho Mirage, August 2001.

40 Andy Neumann, "The Andina Addition." Unpublished manuscript in the collection of Andy Neumann.

1918 Born in Springfield, Missouri

1947 Studied at the Art Center School, Los Angeles, California

1949–1950 Frank Lloyd Wright's Taliesin Fellowship, Scottsdale, Arizona

PROFESSIONAL ASSOCIATIONS
1947 Alvin Lustig, Designer, Los Angeles, California

1954 Welton Becket & Associates, Los Angeles, California

1955–1956 Thornton Ladd, Architect, Pasadena, California

1958–2002 Doetsch, Grether & Cie., Basel, Switzerland

1968–1983 Strässle International, Kirchberg, Switzerland

AWARDS AND GRANTS
1956 Progressive Architecture Design Award for Interiors

1966 Carson Pirie Scott Young Designers Award

1980 Pacifica Award, Los Angeles, California

1980 American Society of Interior Designers (ASID) International Product Design Award

1980 Institute of Business Designs Award

1982–1983 Design Grant, National Endowment for the Arts

1999 Art Center College of Design Certificate of Accomplishment

INDIVIDUAL EXHIBITIONS
1966–1967 *The Furniture Designs of Paul Tuttle*, Pasadena Art Museum, Pasadena, California (catalogue)

1973 *Paul Tuttle,* Esther Bear Gallery, Santa Barbara, California

1973 *Paul Tuttle, 3 Ways,* Galerie im Trudelhaus, Baden, Switzerland

1978 *Paul Tuttle, Designer,* Santa Barbara Museum of Art, Santa Barbara, California (catalogue)

1982 *Paul Tuttle Prototypes,* Carolyn Watson Gallery, Santa Barbara, California

1983 *Paul Tuttle Furniture 1983,* Carolyn Watson Gallery, Santa Barbara, California

1984 *Paul Tuttle Furniture,* Pamela Auchincloss Gallery, Santa Barbara, California

1985 *Paul Tuttle: New Designs/Furniture,* the Design Source, Santa Barbara, California

1987 *Paul Tuttle: Design+ the 80s,* University Art Museum, Santa Barbara, California (catalogue)

1988 *Paul Tuttle: New Furniture/New Space,* the Design Source, Santa Barbara, California

1992 *Paul Tuttle: Recent Work,* Anthony Ralph Gallery, New York, New York

1993 *Paul Tuttle: New Work,* Atelier Richard Tullis, Santa Barbara, California

1995 *Paul Tuttle, 3 Evolutions +,* Contemporary Arts Forum, Santa Barbara, California (catalogue)

1996 *Paul Tuttle: New Work,* Private Exhibition, Santa Barbara, California

1997 *Paul Tuttle: New and Updated Work* (with photographs by Julia Emerson), Private Exhibition, Santa Barbara, California

1998 *Paul Tuttle: New Work Plus* (with paintings by Melissa Chojnackij), Private Exhibition, Santa Barbara, California

2000 *Paul Tuttle: New Works +* (Wayne McCall photographs), Private Exhibition, Santa Barbara, California

2001–2002 *Paul Tuttle Designs,* University Art Museum, Santa Barbara, California

GROUP EXHIBITIONS
1951 *Good Design.* Museum of Modern Art, New York, New York

1951 *Designer-Craftsman Exhibition,* Saint Louis Museum of Art, Saint Louis, Missouri

1955–1956 *California Designed 1955–1956,* Society of Contemporary Designers, Long Beach Municipal Arts Center, Long Beach, California, in collaboration with the M. H. de Young Memorial Museum, San Francisco, California

1960 *Paul Tuttle and Kipp Stewart,* Santa Barbara Museum of Art, Santa Barbara, California

1961 *Arts of Southern California,* Long Beach Museum of Art, Long Beach, California

1962 *California Design/8,* Pasadena Art Museum, Pasadena, California

1964 *Paul Tuttle and Stewart MacDougall: Architectural Furniture,* Felix Landau Gallery, Los Angeles, California

1965 *California Design/9,* Pasadena Art Museum, Pasadena, California

1965 *Paul Tuttle and Stewart MacDougall,* Esther Bear Gallery, Santa Barbara, California

1966 *Design from California,* Carson Pirie Scott & Co., Chicago, Illinois

1968 *California Design/10,* Pasadena Art Museum, Pasadena, California, and *California Exposition,* Sacramento, California

1976 *California Design 76,* Pacific Design Center, Los Angeles, California

1977 *Furniture by Architects—A California View,* Los Angeles County Museum of Art, Los Angeles, California

1981 *Innovative Furniture in America, 1800 to the Present,* Cooper-Hewitt Museum, New York, New York (catalogue)

1982 *Paul Tuttle Furniture, Jesse Alexander Photographs,* Carolyn Watson Gallery, Santa Barbara, California

1986 *"21" Tools for Relaxing,* Copenhagen Fair, Copenhagen, Denmark

1989 *Paul Tuttle: Furniture and Julie Emerson: Photographs,* the Design Source, Santa Barbara, California

1990 *Paul Tuttle and Wayne McCall: New Work,* the Design Source, Santa Barbara, California

1991 *Paul Tuttle and William Prindle: Current Work,* Reynolds Gallery, Westmont College, Santa Barbara, California

1998 *Modern and Beyond: Selections from the Los Angeles County Museum of Art,* Pacific Design Center, Feldman Gallery, West Hollywood, California

2000–2001 *Made in California: Art, Image, and Identity, 1900–2000,* Los Angeles County Museum of Art, Los Angeles, California

View of exhibition installation,
Paul Tuttle Designs, 2001
University Art Museum, UCSB

Paul Tuttle with Isabelle Greene
Landscape renovation of private estate,
Carpinteria, California, 1994 (see p. 116)

BIBLIOGRAPHY

Ames, Richard, "Furniture Viewed as Art Objects in Tuttle Show," *Santa Barbara News-Press* (January 21, 1978).

Andree, Herb, *Santa Barbara Architecture, from Spanish Colonial to Modern* (Santa Barbara, California: Capra Press, 1995), 230–232, 274.

Betsky, Aaron, "The Work of Paul Tuttle in Context," in *Paul Tuttle: 3 Evolutions +* (Santa Barbara, California: Santa Barbara Contemporary Arts Forum, 1995), 1–9.

Berns, Marla. *Paul Tuttle Designs* (Santa Barbara, California: University Art Museum, University of California, Santa Barbara, 2001).

Burnham, Ann, "hot seats," *Abridged (A Publication for the Art Center College of Design Alumni Association)* 3 (Fall 1992): 1, 4.

Darling, Michael, "The Chairman of the Board," *Santa Barbara News-Press* (November 17, 1995).

Di Noto, Andrea, *Art Plastic: Designed for Living* (New York: Abbeville Press, 1984).

Dreyfuss, John, "Architects Sitting Pretty," *Los Angeles Times* (March 3, 1977).

Drohojowska, Hunter, "Design Dialogue: Paul Tuttle; Suave Furniture that Blends Fantasy and Technology," *Architectural Digest* 47 (February 1990): 122–130.

Every, Mary, "No Compromise for Designer of Contemporary Furniture," *Santa Barbara News-Press* (December 1, 1973).

Firlotte, Gregory, "Paul Tuttle: Man of Ideas," *Designers West* 34 (June 1987): 116.

Frank, Steven, "Playful Ingenuity," *Metropolis* 12 (March 1993): 44–47, 61–67.

Gebhard, David, "Paul Tuttle in the Eighties," *Paul Tuttle: Design+ the 80s* (Santa Barbara, California: University Art Museum, University of California, 1987), 6–8.

Gilbar, Anne, "The Architects at Home, Part I," *Santa Barbara Magazine* 7 (spring 1981): 53–58.

Greenberg, Cara, *Op to Pop: Furniture of the 1960s* (Boston: Little, Brown & Company, 1999), 48–49.

Hanks, David A., *Innovative Furniture in America from 1800 to the Present* (New York: Horizon Press, 1981), 119–120.

Havas, Valerie, "Paul Tuttle's Furniture with 10-Speeds," *Santa Barbara Magazine* (May/June 1983).

Heeger, Susan, "Second Nature," *Los Angeles Times Magazine* (February 22, 1998).

King, Carol Soucek, "Contemporary? If You Can Define It, Maybe You're Not," *Designers West* 28.8 (June 1981): 181.

_____, *Furniture: Architects' and Designers' Originals* (New York: Glen Cove, 1994), 33.

Klein, Hilary Dole, "Sitting Pretty," *The Independent* (March 26, 1987).

Jackson, Beverley, "Tuttle's Designs Furnish Material for Exhibition," *Santa Barbara News-Press* (April 24, 1984).

Johnson, Beverly, "The Designer Speaks," *Los Angeles Times* (December 4, 1966).

Leccese, Michael, "Opposites Attract," *Landscape-Architecture* 86 (May 1996): 30–37.

MacMasters, Dan, "Mesa Magic by Paul Tuttle," *Los Angeles Times* (January 15, 1978).

McDonough, Michael, and Gere Kavanaugh, "A Secret History of Design in Los Angeles," *I. D.: The International Design Magazine* 41 (March/April 1994).

Moore, Eudorah M., *The Furniture Designs of Paul Tuttle* (Pasadena, California: Pasadena Art Museum, 1966).

_____, *Paul Tuttle, Designer* (Santa Barbara, California: Santa Barbara Museum of Art, 1978).

"Noted Designer to Appear in L.A. Symposium," *Santa Barbara News-Press* (March 15, 1981).

Owyang, Judy, "Art Invades the Furniture Field," *Santa Monica Evening Outlook* (November 17, 1973).

"Paul Tuttle, An Interview," *Designers West* (February 1974): 82–84.

"Paul Tuttle's 'Cerebrated Solutions'," *Interiors* 126 (February 1967): 16.

Riley, Elizabeth, "Paul Tuttle, Peripatetic," *Artline* 2 (spring 1983): 6–7.

S., V., "Paul Tuttle Designs," *Designers West* (November 1966).

Seldis, Henry J., "A Beach Pavilion by Paul Tuttle," *Art in America* 49, no. 2 (1961): 78–79.

Slavin, Maeve, "Paul Tuttle Out in the Open," *Interiors* 65 (August 1980): 52–53, 82.

Slesin, Suzanne, "Furniture Show: Storage Innovations," *New York Times* (October 30, 1980).

Vogl, Angeline, "Paul Tuttle at Play," *Designers West* 40 (February 1993): 6.

_____, "Chair Man," *Santa Barbara Magazine* 17 (September/October 1991): 9.

von Blunck, Kirk, "An Experiment of Ideas: Paul Tuttle," *Iowa Architect* 38 (winter 1989): 6–9.

W., D., "Paul Tuttle," *House Beautiful* 108 (October 1966): 222–223, 270.

Wettstein-Szakall, Kay, "Architekt und Designer Paul Tuttle: Diese Landschaft ist meine Muse," *Ideales Heim: Das Schwitzer Wohnmagazin* (January 1986): 18–23.

_____, "Architekt und Designer Paul Tuttle: Diese Landschaft ist meine Muse," *Ideales Heim: Wohnmagazin International* (October/November/December 1986): 162–167.

"Young Man on a Mountain," *House Beautiful* 107 (July 1965): 62.

PHOTOGRAPHY CREDITS

Jesse Alexander—1.28; Artek, Helsinki—2.24; Farshid Assassi/copyright 2003—half-title; title; 1.1; 1.4; 1.16a,b–1.19; 1.23; 1.25; 1.30–1.32; 1.41; 1.44; 1.47; 1.48; 1.50; 1.51; 1.53–1.57; 1.59; 1.63a–c; 1.64a,b; 1.66a,b–1.69; 1.71; 1.73; 1.74; 1.76–1.93; 1.95–1.99; 1.101–1.104; 1.106–1.122; 2.1; 2.5; 2.7; 2.11; 2.14; 2.18; 2.19; 2.22; 2.26; 2.28; 2.29; 2.31–2.35; 3.16; 3.25; 3.26a,b; 3.27; pp. 185, 186, 188; Elmer L. Astlef, photograph courtesy of Herman Miller—2.10; Robert Emmett Bright/ *Architectural Digest*, Condé Nast Publications, Inc.—1.62; Jay Connor—3.4; Danforth-Tidmarsh—1.21; 1.22 [from Eudorah Moore, *The Furniture Designs of Paul Tuttle* (Pasadena: Pasadena Art Museum, 1966/1967), fig. 15]; Ellerbe Becket Associates, Minneapolis—3.7; Murray Garrett for Graphic Press, *Time* 51 (March 1, 1949): 78—3.6; Knoll, Inc.—2.8; Thornton Ladd, Ojai—3.8; Wayne McCall—1.24; 1.40; 1.70; 1.72; 1.123; 3.1; 3.12; 3.15; 3.17–3.21; 3.23; 3.24; Grant Mudford—3.29; Museum of Contemporary Art, Los Angeles, Courtesy of Donald Young Gallery, Chicago—2.17; Digital image © The Museum of Modern Art, NY / Licensed by SCALA/ Art Resource, NY—2.23; New Directions—3.3; Helmut Newton—2.25; Elliot Noyce, "Charles Eames," *Art & Architecture* 63

(September 1946): 31—3.5; David Parry, ed., *Thornton Ladd & Associates, Architects* (n.d.), 16—1.29; Philadelphia Museum of Art—1.7; 2.4; 2.6; 2.30; Marvin Rand—1.13, 1.14; Santa Barbara Museum of Art—1.8a,b; 2.5; Julius Shulman—3.2; 3.28; Ezra Stoller © Esto—1.10; 3.9; 3.10; 3.11 [all from David Parry, ed., *Thornton Ladd & Associates, Architects* (n.d.), 41, 10, 5, 57; Strässle International—1.33–1.40; 1.42; 1.43; 1.45; 1.46; 1.49; Tri-Graphic Photography, Pasadena—1.5; Hans van Nes—1.12; Vitra Design Museum—1.52; 1.105; 2.2; 2.3; 2.9; 2.12; 2.13; 2.15; 2.16; 2.21; 2.27

Printed and bound in Germany by Cantz

Design: Lorraine Wild and Robert Ruehlman
Manuscript editing: Lynne Kostman

LIBRARY OF CONGRESS CATALOGING-IN-PUBLICATION DATA

Berns, Marla.
Paul Tuttle designs / Marla C. Berns : with contributions by Michael Darling, Kurt Helfrich
p. cm.
Includes bibliographical references.
ISBN 0-942006-72-0
1. Tuttle, Paul—Criticism and interpretation. 2. Design—United States—History—20th century. I. Tuttle, Paul. II. Darling, Michael. III. Helfrich, Kurt Gerard Frederick. IV. Title.

NK1412.T87B47 2003
749.2'13—dc21   2003051394

Crane Lamp, 1973
Molded plastic, wire, steel plate
Produced by Strässle International, Switzerland